RAND NATIONAL DEFENSE RESEARCH INSTITUTE

Defining Second Generation Open Source Intelligence (OSINT) for the Defense Enterprise

Heather J. Williams, Ilana Blum

Prepared for the Office of the Secretary of Defense
Approved for public release; distribution unlimited

For more information on this publication, visit www.rand.org/t/RR1964

Library of Congress Control Number: 2018943942

ISBN: 978-0-8330-9883-2

Published by the RAND Corporation, Santa Monica, Calif.

Preface

This Research Report discusses the current state of open source intelligence (OSINT) and relevant issues for the defense intelligence enterprise. The work is intended to benefit intelligence practitioners who wish to understand more about open-source analysis and tools. The intricacies and challenges outlined here should be of interest not only to the U.S. Intelligence Community but globally as well, given the Internet's worldwide presence and many manifestations. Although the descriptions provided and the challenges discussed here may be very familiar to those involved in the use of OSINT, they are intended to help others outside of that community understand and access it.

This research was conducted within the Cyber and Intelligence Policy Center of the RAND National Defense Research Institute, a federally funded research and development center sponsored by the Office of the Secretary of Defense, the Joint Staff, the Unified Combatant Commands, the Navy, the Marine Corps, the defense agencies, and the defense Intelligence Community.

For more information on the RAND Cyber and Intelligence Policy Center, see www.rand.org/nsrd/ndri/centers/intel.html or contact the director (contact information is provided on the webpage).

Contents

Figures

Figures

Summary

Although the Intelligence Community (IC) has been involved in open source intelligence (OSINT) for more than 50 years, the definition of OSINT and how it is characterized as an intelligence discipline are still subject to debate. In a 2011 document issued by the Office of the Director of National Intelligence, OSINT was defined as "intelligence produced from publicly available information that is collected, exploited, and disseminated in a timely manner to an appropriate audience for the purpose of addressing a specific intelligence requirement." The Internet and the rise of social media have made OSINT more complex in terms of both sources and methods. This transformation of OSINT is so significant that this report argues it should be seen as a second generation of OSINT. The report provides a definition for second-generation OSINT and discusses how it differs from the historic practice of OSINT, particularly in relation to the defense enterprise. It defines OSINT as an intelligence discipline and provides subtypes of OSINT specific to second-generation OSINT. It then breaks down OSINT methodology and the operations cycle specific to each of its subtypes, laying out some common difficulties in each and efficiencies provided by new technological advancements. The report next provides information about the tools and methods used for OSINT analysis—particularly in social media—and defines the terminology related to lexical, social network, and geospatial analysis. It also discusses some of the challenges of using commercial off-the-shelf (COTS) technology for OSINT analysis within the U.S. IC. Finally, overall conclusions are presented, along with a discussion of new areas of development related to OSINT and the opportunities and obstacles they could present to open-source operations.

The overlapping nature of OSINT with other intelligence disciplines—such as intelligence from human sources and from intercepted communications—is not unique and does not diminish OSINT's status as an independent intelligence discipline. It is useful to subdivide OSINT into subtypes, primarily based on whether it is institutionally or individually driven. These subtypes enable better description of the OSINT methodology and intelligence cycle, as the requirements and difficulties of this process vary dramatically among subtypes. The OSINT intelligence cycle consists of collection, processing, exploitation, and production. Collection is the acquisition of open source information; processing is the method for validating that information;

exploitation identifies the information's intelligence value; and production conveys that value to IC clients.

Much of the analysis of OSINT leverages COTS tools, particularly for analyzing social media data. However, COTS tools are often tailored for the needs of commercial industry rather than the IC. The tools themselves and the companies producing them also change rapidly, as social media analytics is still a new and rapidly evolving industry. Although information on current COTS tools would help the IC understand their precise capabilities, this information would quickly become out of date. Instead, focusing on the methods used in social media analytics provides a framework against which to weigh emerging technological tools. COTS tools generally provide lexical analysis, network analysis, geospatial analysis, or some combination of these capabilities.

OSINT is often underutilized because of the difficulties in understanding dynamic OSINT sources and methods, particularly social media platforms. It also presents new challenges, including how to protect U.S. persons, manage massive quantities of data, and leverage private-sector tools and entities to the fullest possible extent.[1] The improved definitions of the collection methods and methodologies used to process, exploit, and analyze OSINT provided in this report are intended to help intelligence practitioners systematize the various open-source collection efforts throughout the IC and more fully utilize the intelligence value of OSINT. Studying emerging trends in OSINT and technical capabilities will also position IC entities to cultivate these sources and methods to better suit intelligence requirements.

---

1 In this context, *U.S. persons* refers to the definition established in Executive Order 12333 related to authorized United States intelligence activities. Under this definition, a U.S. person is a citizen of the United States; an alien lawfully admitted for permanent residence; an unincorporated association with a substantial number of members who are citizens of the United States or are aliens lawfully admitted for permanent residence; or a corporation that is incorporated in the United States.

Acknowledgments

The authors would like to thank the leaders of the Intelligence Policy Center, who made it possible to undertake this research. We thank RAND researchers working on open-source analysis, including Elizabeth Bodine-Baron, William Marcellino, Michael Decker, Madeline Magnuson, and Zev Winkelman, for their assistance in understanding methods and platforms. Further thanks are due to Sarah Soliman and Mary Quinn for their creative and constructive comments in quality assurance review. In particular, we owe a debt of gratitude to Cameron Colquhoun for his time and expertise in research and review and for providing a ready sounding board for ideas. Finally, we thank Dori Walker for her help with graphics and Holly Johnson for her help throughout the preparation of this report.

Abbreviations

CIA	Central Intelligence Agency
COTS	commercial off-the-shelf
DDI	Directorate for Digital Innovation
DIA	Defense Intelligence Agency
DNI	Director of National Intelligence
DoD	U.S. Department of Defense
DOSC	Defense Open Source Council
ELINT	electronics intelligence
FBIS	Foreign Broadcast Information Service
FBMS	Foreign Broadcast Monitoring Service
GEOINT	geospatial intelligence
GPS	Global Positioning System
HUMINT	human intelligence
IC	Intelligence Community
IMINT	imagery intelligence
INT	intelligence discipline
IP	individual protocol
ISIS	Islamic State of Iraq and al-Sham

MASINT	measurement and signature intelligence
NGA	National Geospatial-Intelligence Agency
NSA	National Security Agency
ODNI	Office of the Director of National Intelligence
OSC	Open Source Center
OSE	Enterprise
OSIF	open source information
OSINT	open source intelligence
OUSD-I	Office of the Under Secretary of Defense for Intelligence
PAI	publicly available information
SIGINT	signals intelligence

CHAPTER ONE

Introduction

The Aims of This Research

The value of open source information (OSIF) to supplement classified intelligence has long been recognized, but the growing pervasiveness of the Internet and the rise of social media and big data analytics in the past two decades have revolutionized open source intelligence (OSINT). New collection efforts and exploitation activities are bringing valuable, original data sources to the Intelligence Community (IC) and the defense enterprise. Open sources also have the power to replace and/or complement some accesses that were once gained only through more dangerous and costly traditional intelligence-collection platforms.

Although the IC has been involved in OSINT for more than 50 years, the definition of OSINT and how it is characterized as an intelligence discipline are still subject to debate. In a 2011 document issued by the Office of the Director of National Intelligence, OSINT was defined as "intelligence produced from publicly available information that is collected, exploited, and disseminated in a timely manner to an appropriate audience for the purpose of addressing a specific intelligence requirement."[1] The Internet and the rise of social media have further complicated this issue. OSINT is becoming more complex in terms of both sources and methods. Individuals are making information available in ways that never existed before, including online expressions of personal sentiment, photographs of local places and happenings, and publicized social and professional networks. Compounding computer power and data-science techniques allow for the retention and processing of mass quantities of publicly available data. Machine learning, computer algorithms, and automated reasoning further expand the capacity to process this information and find implications that are of intelligence value.

These new methods and systems also necessitate a high level of technical knowledge for collectors obtaining and analysts processing publicly available information. The historic business of OSINT was primarily translation—making foreign news articles accessible to all-source intelligence analysts. Once a largely original open-source

---

1 Office of the Director of National Intelligence, *U.S. National Intelligence: An Overview 2011*, Washington, D.C., 2011, p. 54.

report was translated, all-source analysts could generally incorporate it into a finished intelligence product. The modern business of OSINT often requires more-extensive acquisition, processing, and exploitation to produce an open-source product that can then be integrated into a finished all-source product. Additionally, information often comes from individuals, which introduces new complexities for the IC in protecting the privacy of U.S. persons. All these changes necessitate a more robust definition of OSINT, as open-source data can come in many forms.

In view of the changing nature of publicly available information, we suggest that the current period should be considered the second generation of OSINT. Practitioners recognized that the rise of personal computing in the 1990s—also the period in which the acronym OSINT was coined—would have a huge impact. Incidents such as the Iranian Green Revolution in 2009 provided a vivid example of how using new forms of social media could provide a real-time intelligence picture in a denied environment.[2] However, we recommend dating the shift to second-generation OSINT to 2005. It was in 2005 that the IC created the Open Source Center.[3] The Internet was also changing during this period, with the bulk of online content shifting to dynamic web pages, user-generated content, and social media. This transition is often described as the emergence of Web 2.0, a term popularized at the Web 2.0 Conference in late 2004.[4] Facebook.com and YouTube.com launched in 2005, and Twitter was founded in early 2006.[5]

This report provides definitions of second-generation OSINT and the OSINT process. This information should help intelligence consumers better understand OSINT collection and analytic methods, aid the organization of OSINT efforts, and codify the working lexicon used by open-source practitioners. The report also describes some of the rapidly changing tools available for analyzing online material, particularly social media content.

In conducting this research, we reviewed literature on the practice of OSINT and examined definitions used in other areas by the IC in the context of modern OSIF sources. This effort relied on declassified material on the Central Intelligence Agency's (CIA's) website; unclassified articles in *Studies in Intelligence*, an IC-published journal for intelligence professionals; and textbooks on intelligence used by IC members and students. Given our intent to keep this study unclassified, we limited our research to

---

2 Cameron Colquhoun, "A Brief History of Open Source Intelligence," *Bellingcat*, July 14, 2016.

3 Central Intelligence Agency, "Establishment of the DNI Open Source Center," *News and Information*, November 8, 2005.

4 Tim O'Reilly, "What Is Web 2.0: Design Patterns and Business Models for the Next Generation of Software," *O'Reilly*, September 30, 2005.

5 Facebook was founded in 2004 at Harvard University but was available only for student use at that time. Facebook purchased its current URL, facebook.com, in 2005 and was made available to those without a .edu email address in 2006.

publicly available documentation, which is a small subset of information available to the IC. A more comprehensive study of this topic would benefit greatly from an extensive data-collection effort with OSINT practitioners and experts.

An improved definition of the collection methods and methodologies used to process, exploit, and analyze OSINT can help intelligence practitioners systematize the various open-source collection efforts through the IC, evaluate OSIF, and integrate OSINT into all-source intelligence products. OSINT is often underutilized by the IC because of the difficultly in understanding emerging OSINT sources and methods, particularly social media platforms. All-source analysts sometimes fail to exploit these data sources to the fullest because of their uncertainty about how to evaluate the credibility and reliability of the information and their desire to protect personally identifiable information and U.S. persons' data. Analysts may also be further hesitant to fully embrace social media given personal unfamiliarity with the platforms, as intelligence professionals are often counseled to maintain a low social media profile. Finally, transmitting source material to IC systems makes leveraging some open-source material just one extra step that may slow down the acquisition and analysis. Conversely, the high production value of some social media analysis may result in it being presented as a stand-alone intelligence deliverable to customers, when an all-source context could have provided a more comprehensive intelligence picture.

Some previous efforts to define OSINT have focused on how to define OSIF and publicly available information (PAI)—the source material. The resulting definitions focused on characterizing the raw information collected without considering the use of classified methods and technical means. In Chapter Two, we look comprehensively at OSINT as an intelligence discipline that includes methods of acquiring, processing, exploiting, and analyzing information. In Chapter Three, we focus on the methods of open-source analysis, particularly in the realm of social media data. Finally, Chapter Four briefly discusses some of the emerging challenges and opportunities presented by OSINT.

For IC practitioners immersed in the world of OSINT, the material presented here may not be new. However, our goal is to provide context and definitions that will enable other IC members to better understand the work of their OSINT-focused counterparts and the value it can provide to intelligence support to policymakers. We hope that such grounding will aid their efforts to incorporate OSINT material into intelligence products and will put greater value on the technical skills possessed by OSINT practitioners. Further, it could enhance their appreciation of the potential intelligence value of OSIF. This report should also be of use to those outside the IC who may wish to understand more about OSINT, how it can be used to enhance intelligence products, and the challenges and gaps encountered by professionals in this field.

A Brief History of OSINT and Its Relationship to the Defense Enterprise

OSINT began as a defense-oriented enterprise. The United States established the Foreign Broadcast Monitoring Service (FBMS) on February 26, 1941, to monitor and analyze the propaganda programs of the Axis powers.[6] Initially operated by the Federal Communications Commission—the only organization with the capabilities to perform the mission—it was financed with special defense appropriations.[7] On July 26, 1942, FBMS was renamed the Federal Broadcast Information Service (FBIS), partly to make it sound more like a war agency.[8] Nearly shuttered at the end of World War II, FBIS was taken over by the War Department on January 1, 1946.[9] It was transferred to the CIA a year later under the National Security Act of 1947, by which time it was already an "almost mature, trained and disciplined" organization from the war experience. Twenty years later, the CIA's official history of FBIS described "its fundamental organization and responsibilities . . . basic operation and methods" as largely unchanged.[10]

From the creation of FBIS until the 1990s, the purview of open-source analysis within the IC was primarily monitoring and translating foreign-press sources. There are some important differences between this historic character of OSINT—the first generation of OSINT—and today's second generation. Collection of material was a significant emphasis of the first-generation OSINT effort. FBIS operated 20 worldwide bureaus to allow it to physically collect material for exploitation. Embassies also provided a platform for collection of material. In addition to diplomatic officers, defense attachés served as overt collectors. The Defense Attaché System was consolidated in 1964–1965 under the authorities of the Defense Intelligence Agency (DIA).[11] Some mission functions were reduced in order to focus on high-priority material, but the remaining requirement to process this material was primarily translation; although, it should be noted that FBIS has served some analytic functions—primarily trend analysis—since its founding.[12]

---

[6] Joseph E. Roop, *Foreign Broadcast Information Service History.* Part I: *1941–1947*, Central Intelligence Agency, April 1969, p. 7.

[7] Roop, 1969, p. 8.

[8] Roop, 1969, p. 50.

[9] Roop, 1969, pp. 278–279.

[10] Roop, 1969, p. 1.

[11] Deane J. Allen and Brian G. Shellum (eds.), *Defense Intelligence Agency: At the Creation, 1961–1965*, Defense Intelligence Agency, January 2002.

[12] J. Niles Riddel, *Remarks at the First International Symposium, 'National Security and National Competitiveness: Open Source Solutions,'* Open Source Solutions, Inc., December 2, 1992.

FBIS's work provided critical insights and decision points for the military during the Cold War, including the first indications of the Soviet removal of missiles from Cuba, early warning of the Soviet withdrawal from Afghanistan, and context on crises in Hungary and Czechoslovakia. Eighty percent of the information used to monitor the collapse of the Soviet Union has been attributed to open sources.[13] The end of the Cold War resulted in budget cuts for most IC institutions, but it created a particular crisis for FBIS and the open-source mission. At the same time the volume of OSIF was increasing dramatically, FBIS was rapidly losing resources. In 1997, FBIS was at risk of dissolution as part of CIA budget cuts but was saved by a public campaign led by the Federation of American Scientists.[14] FBIS was described by academicians at the time as the "biggest bang for the buck in the American intelligence community."[15]

Leaders in the IC recognized that the challenges and dynamics of the 21st century would bring more demand for OSINT, not less. FBIS Deputy Director J. Niles Riddel, at the First International Symposium on Open Source in 1992, acknowledged changes in OSINT resulting from the rise of personal computing, large-capacity digital storage, capable search engines, and broadband communication networks. He believed all these factors would lead to exponential growth in the commercialization of information.[16] At the same event, then-CIA Deputy Director Admiral William Studeman called for "a revolutionary change in the Intelligence Community's approach to open-source management, collection, processing and dissemination."[17]

The IC leaders saw that open source was becoming an unwieldy intelligence discipline. Admiral Studeman described other collection disciplines as "highly structured" but declared that "open source is not a tightly integrated discipline" and that "open source information collectors, processors, and users have been diverse and decentralized groups spread across the breadth and depth of the Community." The IC did not have knowledge of its own unclassified holdings and capabilities, and it had no means for sharing OSIF.

These problems were particularly acute in the defense enterprise. A working group at the Office of the Under Secretary of Defense for Intelligence (OUSD-I) in 2004 found deficiencies in open-source policy and doctrine, training, and management. Furthermore, U.S. Department of Defense (DoD) open-source requirements

---

[13] Admiral William Studeman, *Teaching the Giant to Dance: Contradictions and Opportunities in Open Source Within the Intelligence Community*, Open Source Solutions, Inc., December 1992.

[14] Ben Barber, "CIA Media Translations May Be Cut: Users Rush to Save Valuable Resource," *Washington Times*, December 30, 1996.

[15] Norman Kempster, "Academia Mounts Fight to Save a CIA Program," *Los Angeles Times*, January 14, 1997.

[16] Riddel, 1992.

[17] Studeman, 1992.

were underrepresented and underfunded within the IC.[18] These findings prompted the establishment of the Defense Open Source Council (DOSC), which was appointed as the primary government mechanism for DoD OSINT through DoD Instruction 3115.12.[19] This DoD Instruction is in the process of being updated to take into account a number of the trends and challenges described in this report.

On November 1, 2005, the Director of National Intelligence (DNI) created the Open Source Center (OSC) and designated the CIA as its executive agent, later redesignating it as the "functional manager."[20] Based at the CIA and replacing FBIS, the OSC brand gave OSINT practitioners greater license to expand beyond news monitoring and translation. The creation of the OSC fulfilled a requirement of the Intelligence Reform and Terrorism Prevention Act of 2004, which specifically called for the creation of an intelligence center dedicated to "the collection, analysis, production, and dissemination of open-source intelligence."[21] The DNI is charged with ensuring that OSIF and analysis is effectively and efficiently used by the IC. In addition to OSINT production, the OSC's objectives include training in open-source exploitation and analysis, development of tools, and testing of new technologies.[22]

In October 2015, the OSC was renamed the Open Source Enterprise (OSE), and it was brought under a newly created Directorate for Digital Innovation (DDI) within the CIA.[23] The inclusion of the OSE in a directorate focused on cyber threats and digital technology could enhance the institution's embrace of technology and analytic tools; however, some worry that it could also hamper the outward orientation of the organization's collection and analysis mission in support of the entire IC.[24] Further, the Office of the Director of National Intelligence (ODNI) acknowledges that "open-source collection responsibilities are broadly distributed through the IC," describing the OSC as a major, but not the only, collector of OSIF.[25]

---

[18] Craig Manley, "Managing Army Open Source Activities," *Military Intelligence Professional Bulletin*, October–December 2005, p. 10.

[19] U.S. Department of Defense, *Department of Defense Instruction 3115.12*, August 24, 2010.

[20] Intelligence Community Directive 301 uses the term "executive agent," but functional manager is more commonly used now. See Director of National Intelligence, "National Open Source Enterprise," Intelligence Community Directive Number 301, effective July 11, 2006.

[21] Intelligence Reform and Terrorism Prevention Act of 2004, Sec. 1052, pp. 166–167.

[22] *The Director of National Intelligence Open Source Center Implementation Plan*, November 1, 2005.

[23] "Deputy Director Cohen Delivers Remarks on CIA of the Future at Cornell University," *News and Information*, Central Intelligence Agency, September 17, 2015.

[24] Stephen Slick, "Measuring Change at the CIA," *Foreign Policy*, May 4, 2016.

[25] Office of the Director of National Intelligence, "What Is Intelligence?" undated.

CHAPTER TWO

Rethinking OSINT as an Intelligence Discipline

The ODNI defines six collection disciplines, or six basic intelligence sources.[1] OSINT is included in the ODNI's categories, but other sources challenge its inclusion as an intelligence discipline (INT). Some reject OSINT because information from open sources is not collected clandestinely. Alternatively, Mark Lowenthal, formerly Vice Chairman of the National Intelligence Council, argues that OSINT is not a separate intelligence discipline but is a facet of each of the various other intelligence disciplines.[2] Lowenthal would shift the definitions of INTs toward the type of information collected, rather than the traditional focus on the manner of acquisition. Stephen Mercado in *Studies in Intelligence* similarly describes "open versions of the covert arts of, overhead imagery [intelligence] (IMINT), and signals intelligence (SIGINT)."[3] How intelligence disciplines are defined is important, because the definitions often dictate how intelligence information is treated by all-source intelligence analysts, particularly how it is evaluated for credibility and validity. They also affect whether an intelligence product is considered single-source or all-source, which impacts the IC's assessments about the reliability of the product. Furthermore, prioritization of collection efforts in the way intelligence is classified (and therefore shared and disseminated) often follows the definitions of intelligence disciplines, underlining how critical it is to characterize OSINT.

These definitional issues are compounded by the fact that some intelligence professionals tend to think of INTs as unique and distinct from each other. A more effective framework would be to think of these disciplines as overlapping, as Lowenthal's and Mercado's definitional frameworks do. Intelligence disciplines are rarely completely independent of each other, and definitions of them are sometimes driven more by the unique regulatory authorities of intelligence collection agencies than by distinct differences between the collection methods or the material itself. For example, the line

[1] Office of the Director of National Intelligence, undated.

[2] Mark M. Lowenthal, "OSINT: The State of the Art, The Artless State," *Studies in Intelligence*, Vol. 45, No. 3, 2001, released September 5, 2014, p. 63.

[3] Stephen C. Mercado, "Sailing the Sea of OSINT in the Information Age," *Studies in Intelligence*, Vol. 48, No. 3, 2004.

between geospatial intelligence (GEOINT) and measurement and signature intelligence (MASINT) is frequently blurred and is becoming more so by advanced imagery techniques. Similarly, electronics intelligence (ELINT) is sometimes considered MASINT and sometimes considered a component of SIGINT. HUMINT is sometimes characterized in ways similar to SIGINT.

OSINT may provide the most-complex and most-frequent instances of these types of disciplinary overlap, but it is not unique among intelligence disciplines in doing so. Increasingly, GEOINT is also OSINT, as commercial satellites are now capable of providing an overhead imagery capability on a par with the capability historically provided only by classified collection platforms. OSINT derived from social media could be considered a type of HUMINT and SIGINT. Similar to HUMINT, social media data collection provides insights and perspectives of an individual—one who either has unique access or may provide a representative point of view for a community or specific national population. Similar to SIGINT, social media data collection may involve electronic collection of a massive number of records that are sifted using technical means to identify interactions or communications of critical interest. Moreover, as information on the Internet increasingly is secured—and encryption becomes more pervasive, accessible, and robust—information that would have been openly publicly available just a few years ago may now be accessible only by using clandestine or covert collection methods. The implication of this trend is that more OSIF may be more difficult to obtain via open-source collection methods.

Figure 2.1 provides a visual representation of these overlapping intelligence disciplines. It does not purport to indicate all the ways in which intelligence disciplines could potentially overlap; rather, it illustrates the blurring lines between different intelligence areas.

Defining Open Source and OSINT

We define OSINT as publicly available information that has been discovered, determined to be of intelligence value, and disseminated by a member of the IC. This is consistent with the U.S. definition in Section 931 of Public Law 109-163 that defines OSINT as "intelligence that is produced from publicly available information and is collected, exploited, and disseminated in a timely manner to an appropriate audience for the purpose of addressing a specific intelligence requirement."[4] OSIF is merely unclassified data available to the public, while OSINT results from applying processing and exploiting the information to validate it as relevant, accurate, and actionable for use by the consumers.

[4] Public Law 109-163, National Defense Authorization Act for Fiscal Year 2006, Sec. 931, Department of Defense Strategy for Open-Source Intelligence, January 6, 2006.

Figure 2.1
The Overlapping Nature of Intelligence Disciplines

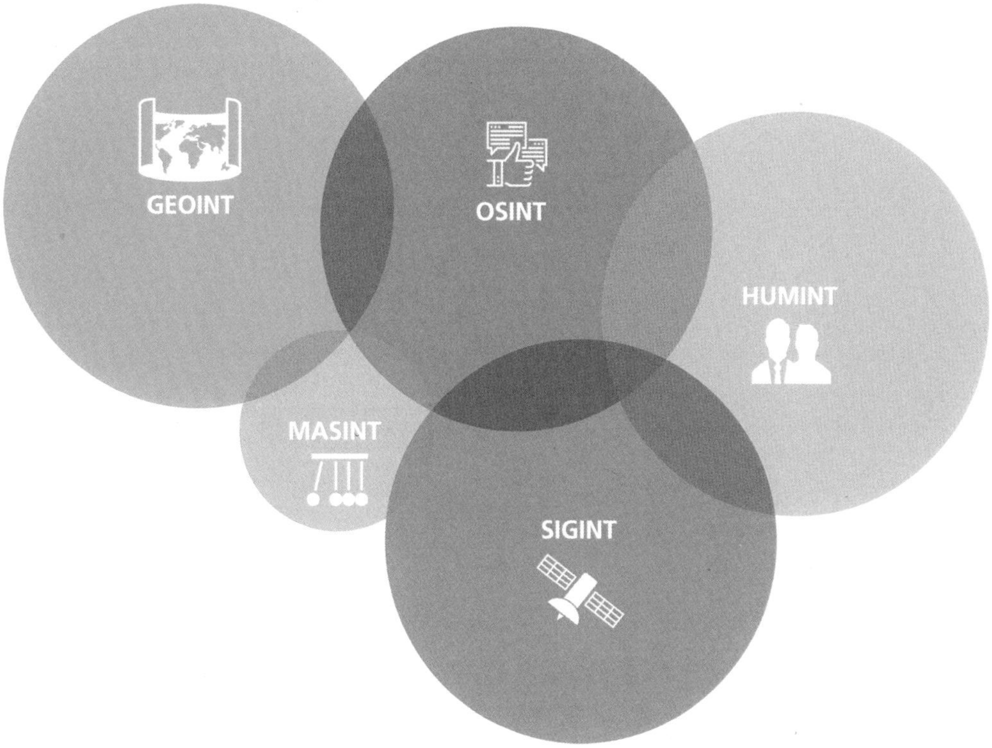

SOURCE: RAND analysis.
RAND *RR1964-2.1*

What constitutes OSINT and OSIF is not universally defined. For example, the *Handbook of Intelligence Studies*, a popular intelligence textbook, identifies four distinct categories of OSIF and OSINT. Open-source data are defined as raw print, broadcast, oral debriefing, or other forms of information from a primary source. OSIF is described as data that can be put together from generic information that is typically widely disseminated; sources include newspapers, books, broadcasts, and general daily reports. OSINT is defined as information that has been "deliberated, discovered, discriminated, distilled, and disseminated to a select audience."[5] Validated OSINT is distinguished from OSINT by the high degree of validity and certainty associated with it. These definitions, however, are of only limited utility to intelligence professionals. For example, would an Associated Press news article be considered open-source data (since it is raw print) or OSIF (since it could be printed in a newspaper)? We have adjusted and expanded upon these definitions to better distinguish between these types and

[5] Loch K. Johnson, ed., *Handbook of Intelligence Studies*, New York: Routledge, 2007, p. 132.

to draw more directly on some of the definitions provided by the IC. We have also refrained from using the term *validated OSINT,* as validity of intelligence information is best understood on a spectrum rather than as a binary measure.

We propose the following typology:

- Open-source data are material that would be of little individual value in isolation but is of intelligence value in compilation. For example, a single Twitter tweet reflecting a random individual's view on the Islamic State of Iraq and al-Sham (ISIS) is of almost no intelligence value; however, synthesizing all the tweets on views of ISIS within a geographic area is of great intelligence value. Similarly, individual protocol (IP) addresses are of no intelligence value, but mapping the world's 4.3 billion IP addresses provides a global picture of Internet usage.[6] Open-source data include public material that is not explicitly published but is still publicly or commercially available, such as commercial satellite imagery.
- OSIF is material that can be lawfully obtained through request, purchase, or observation by a member of the public.[7] This includes open-source data but also includes material of more substantive content. OSIF is therefore the most expansive category of publicly or commercially available information.

OSINT Subtypes

One challenge of defining OSIF is the fact that there are few recognized subcategories for distinguishing between types of information, and existing definitions do not accurately capture the changing nature of public information. The definition of gray literature, for example, has been particularly complicated by the advent of the Internet. The U.S. Government's Interagency Gray Literature Work Group in 1995 defined gray literature as "foreign or domestic open-source material that usually is available through specialized channels and may not enter normal channels or systems of publication, distribution, bibliographic control, or acquisition by booksellers or subscription agents."[8] This definition could include a broad array of information types—conference papers, corporate documents, dissertations, government reports, newsletters, trade literature, trip reports—typically published by research establishments, national governments, private publishers, corporations, trade associations and unions, think tanks, and academia. The most difficult aspect of dealing with gray literature in the past was

[6] Darla Cameron and Nancy Scola, "Mapping the World's 4.3 Billion Internet Addresses," *Washington Post,* January 7, 2015.

[7] *Intelligence Community Directive Number 301: National Open Source Enterprise,* July 11, 2006; Joint Publication 2-0: Joint Intelligence, October 22, 2013.

[8] Mason H. Soule and R. Paul Ryan, *Gray Literature,* Defense Technical Information Center, August 10, 1995.

its accessibility, and accessibility continues to underpin current definitions of it.[9] However, much of this material is now available online. Focusing on access, therefore, is no longer an effective criterion for defining gray literature.

The Congressional Research Service in 2007 described four categories of OSIF: "widely available data and information; targeted commercial data; individual experts; and 'gray' literature."[10] These categories, however, are not consistent with the IC conceptualization of open source, nor do they effectively capture social media content. There is obviously a danger in defining OSIF too narrowly, given the rapidly changing nature of online sources and platforms. However, without a framework to differentiate between the broad swaths of OSIF, the OSINT intelligence cycle cannot be defined with precision because of the dramatic differences in the processing and exploitation of different types of OSIF.

We propose dividing OSIF into four categories—two main categories, each bifurcated one level further. These divisions were chosen because they provide some consistency in the requirements to collect, process, and exploit the information. The first differentiation is determined by the content generator: institutionally generated content versus individually generated content. Institutionally generated content consists of news media and other institutional content, much of which may have been previously defined as gray literature. Individually driven content, or social media content, is divided between long-form and short-form, which have important differences for processing and usage.

News Media Content

The content of news media is self-identified and publicly recognized as journalism. Its sources are multimedium—newspapers, journals (both print and online), television, and radio. News media also include news aggregator sites, which may or may not publish original content. News media content includes state-produced content when specifically distributed by a media outlet.

Gray Literature

Gray literature is content that comes from non-media institutions and organizations, both public and private. It includes material from research establishments, national governments, private publishers, corporations, trade associations and unions, think tanks, and academia. An underlying assumption is that most institutional content does not exist only in the virtual space, but that there is generally some brick-and-mortar presence and institutional cohesion. Despite efforts initiated decades ago to

---

[9] Joint Chiefs of Staff, JCAT: *Intelligence Guide for First Responders,* National Counterterrorism Center, 2013.

[10] Richard A. Best, Jr., and Alfred Cumming, *Open Source Intelligence (OSINT): Issues for Congress*, Congressional Research Service, December 2007.

better organize the acquisition, long-term storage, and distribution of gray literature, it is still often collected and used in an ad hoc manner.

Long-Form Social Media Content

Long-form individual-user content is text-heavy material from single individuals or small groups. It includes material from blogs and sites such as Reddit and Tumblr. Much social media content analysis has focused on short-form content, leaving long-form content often underutilized.

Short-Form Social Media Content

Short-form individual-user content is material from platforms such as Facebook, Twitter, and LinkedIn. In contrast to long-form content, short-form content generally has little intelligence value individually; intelligence value is generally gained from the aggregation of such information. An exception exists, however, when short-form social media content is obtained from specific accounts of high interest, for example, accounts of famous individuals such as senior government figures, thought leaders, and prominent journalists. High-value short-form content could also include accounts from individuals who are part of a group being targeted by the IC, such as a special military unit or a militant group.

OSINT Methodology: The OSINT Operations Cycle

Only a portion of the massive volume of OSIF that is disseminated and shared on a daily basis qualifies as information that is relevant, timely, and actionable for an OSINT analyst.[11] Determining what is less or more relevant requires an enormous amount of effort spread across the whole intelligence spectrum, from initial collection through dissemination of findings to the policymaker receiving them. The transformation of information from raw intelligence involves steps critical to providing the context to assess a report's validity and reliability.

OSINT, however, is still in need of a clear methodology.[12] There are a few existing models to describe intelligence methodology. The CIA's intelligence cycle describes this process as planning and direction, collection, processing, analysis and production, and dissemination. The *Handbook of Intelligence Studies* describes these stages as collection, processing, analysis and production, classification, and dissemination.

---

[11] Libor Benes, "OSINT, New Technologies, Education: Expanding Opportunities and Threats. A New Paradigm," *Journal of Strategic Security*, Vol. 6, No. 5, Fall 2013, p. 25.

[12] Lowenthal, 2014.

In the context of OSINT, we focus on four key steps: collection, processing, exploitation, and production, as shown in Figure 2.2.[13] (Processing and exploitation may not happen completely sequentially, but rather in parallel or in concert.) In the simplest terms, these stages can be described as acquiring information, validating that information, identifying the value of the information, and providing the information to customers. In the sections below, we break down each of these areas into component parts. We will do so specific to each of the types of OSINT rather than generalize the stage for all types of open-source material.

We roughly characterize the difficulty of each component of the methodological cycle as easy, medium, or hard for each of the OSINT subtypes (see Figure 2.3). In characterizing difficulty, we considered factors that contribute to the difficulty level, such as labor hours, computing resources needed, and access to hard targets; however, we did not have the resources to develop a complete methodology and systematically compare these factors. Our rough characterizations would almost certainly generate debate among open source professionals. For example, some analysts might argue that the acquisition of social media content is fairly easy, given the easy access to Twitter data. However, many of the IC's hard targets use national platforms, and Twitter usage

Figure 2.2
The OSINT Operations Cycle

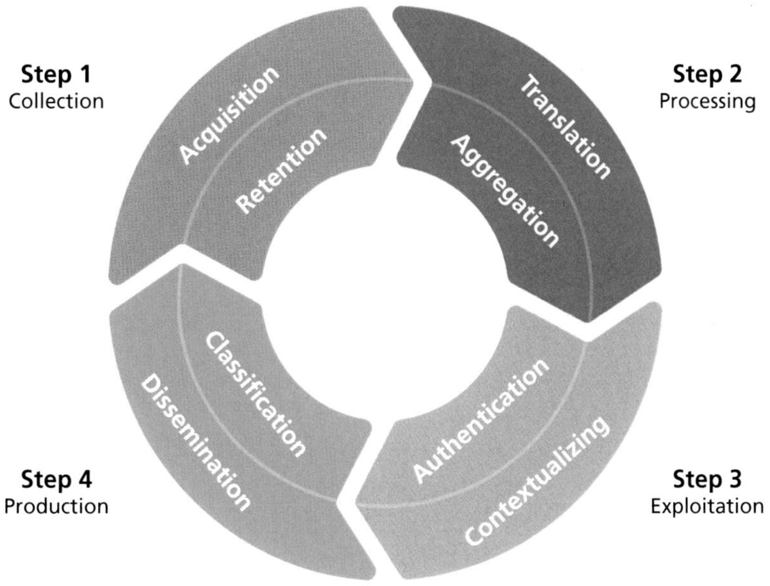

SOURCE: RAND analysis.
RAND *RR1964-2.2*

---

[13] We have chosen to use the terms *exploitation* and *production*, rather than *analysis* and *dissemination* to better differentiate open-source production from all-source analysis.

Figure 2.3
Difficulty of OSINT-Cycle Components, by Type of OSIF

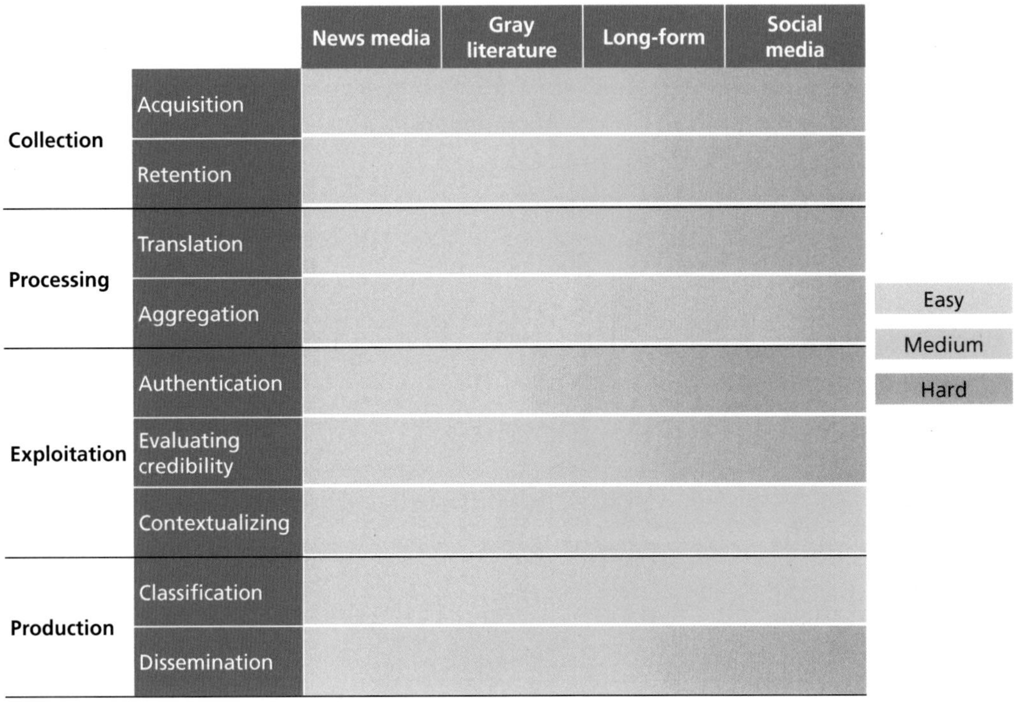

SOURCE: RAND analysis.
RAND *RR1964-2.3*

is banned or limited, so pulling social media content from only this platform would not answer many IC requirements. It would be useful for the IC to do a more rigorous review of how time- and skill-intensive each of these areas is for each subtype of OSINT, as this could inform a more precise division of resources and could help in evaluating the intelligence value gained relative to the effort expended.

Collection

The first stage, collection, includes the identification of potentially useful information and the retention of that material. This stage requires guidance—either explicit or general—for open source collectors to identify the kinds of information that should be collected and to prioritize collection efforts to reflect the requirements of the IC. Acquisition is the physical or electronic collection of this information. Retention is the continued holding of acquired OSIF.

Of the four types of OSIF considered here, news media content is the easiest to collect. For first-generation OSINT, physical acquisition of transmitted news media data presented logistic challenges that required FBIS to disperse to multiple geographic locations to intercept broadcasts. Collection of print material was dependent on the presence of a diplomatic officer or clandestine collector to physically acquire published material. Today, however, with most news media information available online, logistic challenges have shifted from processing to information management. Retention of news media information is fairly simple. The volume of such information is manageable, and the information generally comes in a standardized and text-based format.

Gray literature, like news media content, is becoming easier to collect, for similar reasons. Gray literature creators have been slower than news media in transitioning to online content, so there are still cases in which a collector is required to physically acquire information in hard copy, particularly in the developing world, where Internet usage by institutions may not be widespread. As is the case for news media content, retention of gray literature is not very difficult.

Social media information, in contrast, presents many unique challenges in the collection phase, for both short-form and long-form content. First, a complete picture of the raw data can be difficult to acquire. In the startup phase of social media content analysis, social media analytics were easily accessible and sometimes even free to use. One company, Topsy, for example, provided public access to a complete index of Twitter material since Twitter's start in 2006. However, as social media analytics has become an established industry, platforms like Topsy have been purchased and shuttered by larger companies looking to monetize these markets. Social media aggregation companies that market social media data often provide only a fraction of the data from a social media platform or dataset from only a specific window of time. Furthermore, these providers also tend to focus on social media data from U.S.-based platforms, primarily Twitter and Facebook, although native platforms are more relevant for some of the IC's key interests. In addition, even if the IC can acquire a complete set of social media data rather than a subset, the data do not present a representative sample for a population. Demographic groups do not use social media evenly, and in many locations of interest to the IC, usage can be tremendously impacted by socioeconomic class.

The collection of social media data also raises legal issues related to protection of U.S. persons, which is particularly relevant to retention. Such issues are less present with gray literature and mostly nonexistent with news media. As social media data can easily include data related to U.S. persons, the IC must follow stringent procedures related to the collection and retention of information. Those procedures are detailed in a variety of regulations, including Executive Order 12333 and DoD Directive 5240.01. In addition, both long-form and short-form social media content are more dynamic than news media content or gray literature. A news article (with the exception of corrections) is generally not a living document—if a story has changed, a separate, new article will be generated. In contrast, a discussion trend may garner interest and updates for a few days or weeks, or it could continue for years. Acquisition and retention of social media content, in particular, must be real-time and constant, as impactful content may be posted and removed in a short period of time if it incites controversy or reveals sensitive information—cases that could be of particular interest to the IC. Finally, both long-form and short-form social media content are increasingly presented in formats other than text. YouTube videos are an example of long-form social media content in a different format, and short-form social media data in a nontext format include images on platforms such as Flickr and "live" videos on platforms such as Facebook and Twitter.

Processing

The second phase, processing, involves validating the information and making it usable. Processing can take many forms, including translating source materials from their original language into English and transforming video materials or photographs into usable intelligence. Processing in second-generation OSINT presents a sea change compared to processing in first-generation OSINT, both in changes to existing methods and the requirements of new methods. Many of the tasks accomplished in processing may now be accomplished more readily and at less cost through the use of software programs, including professional-grade versions of Google Translate. At the same time, OSINT now has an abundance of available information in a less-structured format, which makes processing much more involved. We identify two components of processing: translation and aggregation. These components do not necessarily need to occur in a given sequence, although in certain cases one could assist in the other.

Processing of news media data primarily involves translation into English. Once the bulk of the FBIS effort, translation has been radically impacted by the rapid advancement of machine translation, at least for languages in which a common syntax and corpus have been documented. While OSC linguists still have a critical role to

Data Scientists in the IC

The increasing quantity of open-source data and the need for quantitative analytic skills in the processing and exploitation of social media data have driven a discussion about the need for professional data scientists in the IC. The DIA in 2013, for example, initiated a program to modernize defense intelligence analysis partly by enhancing its capacity for data analysis, and it examined how to create a data science capability. A RAND study commissioned by DIA, *Defining the Roles, Responsibilities, and Functions for Data Science Within the Defense Intelligence Agency*, provided recommendations for structuring this data science workforce. The need for data scientists is not unique to open source professionals, however. It generally reflects the increasingly large and diverse array of sensors and the technical ease of capturing and storing large bodies of data. Nevertheless, incorporating greater numbers of data scientists into the IC workforce would have a positive impact on the IC's capabilities to do sophisticated processing and exploitation of open source data.

play—providing nuance and cultural context to foreign-language material—they can now focus their efforts on providing analytic value in the exploitation phase. Machine translation is most efficient for news media content, which uses a standard vocabulary and often follows formulaic structure. Gray literature generally also follows standards of professional writing that would be conducive to machine translation, although the advanced and specific topics covered in gray literature sometimes necessitate human intervention. Social media information has advantages and disadvantages for machine translation. On one hand, social media posts tend to contain a limited number of characters—Twitter, for example, limits users to 140 characters. On the other hand, social media posts are more likely to contain slang, shorthand, and emojis or icons. They also may use multiple languages and probably more frequently contain typographical errors. Whereas long-form social media content may contain enough information to provide some consistent record through which to deduce the style or stance of the author, short-form social media content is less likely to provide such a record unless a body of the material or activity is compiled.

Aggregation, which is generally not necessary for news media data and gray literature, is a critical step for analysis of many types of social media content, particularly short-form social media content. Aggregation may also involve reduction or integration in translating a body of data into a usable form. Many commercial companies provide data aggregation services which eliminate the need for the IC to do direct collection. While these data aggregators can minimize the collection and processing of information, they may not provide data from multiple platforms, and they may not provide full samples of data. It may also be difficult for the IC to know exactly what data have been included in the dataset, which complicates its ability to authenticate the data and put them in an appropriate context.

Exploitation

Exploitation seeks to determine whether the information is what it purports to be and what its value is to the IC. Exploitation is also sometimes referred to as analysis. As former CIA officer and intelligence scholar Arthur Hulnik notes, one of the most significant challenges associated with using OSINT products is the sheer volume of information that is publicly available and the degrees of reliability inherent in that information. Thus, a great deal of time in analyzing OSINT must be spent on separating the reliable, "good" intelligence from the "bad."[14] Analysts must be able to "gather, judge, and sort information, know and handle limitations, and understand different users, needs, tasks, information mix, organization, institutions, and the law."[15] The finished product should provide analytical conclusions guided by the available sources.

---

[14] Arthur S. Hulnick, "The Dilemma of Open Source Intelligence: Is OSINT Really Intelligence?" in Loch K. Johnson, ed., *The Oxford Handbook of National Security Intelligence*, New York: Oxford University Press, 2010.

[15] Benes, 2013, p. 32.

We break exploitation down into three phases: authenticating, evaluating credibility, and contextualizing. Authenticating seeks to verify whether the information is what it says it is. For information coming from institutional sources, this is fairly straightforward. Articles about the *New York Times* have a high probability of being knowingly and purposefully published by the *New York Times*. Likewise, gray literature published by government websites can be assumed with high confidence to have been produced and disseminated by the government. Authentication of social media content is much more difficult. Users may purposefully obfuscate their true identity, or they may provide false information about their identity. This goes beyond simply the user's true name. For example, a person could be dishonest about her or his location or personal attributes. If the IC is attempting to ascertain atmospherics within a country, it is very important that users be within that country rather than members of a diaspora. Authentication may need to occur concurrent with data-aggregation functions to ensure that a data sample or composite is not wrongly skewed.

Evaluating credibility, like authentication, is fairly straightforward for traditional media content and gray literature but extremely difficult for social media content. A credibility measure seeks to determine whether the information is trustworthy—that is, whether it was provided without intent to deny or deceive and whether its source has plausible access to it. The *New York Times*, for example, almost universally publishes material with purpose—it intends its content to be accurate and it is transparent about its sources. This may be less true for foreign media sources, particularly state-run media outlets, that intend to influence or message their populations. However, there is probably a history of material from such sources that could provide some indication as to the credibility of their information.

Unlike news media, social media is generally not secondhand information. The content usually comes directly from the source. However, that is not always the case, and the originality of the source may be suspect. Retweets, reposts, and bots are examples of social media data that have proven important for obfuscating original source intentions. Even if a source is providing information on an event he or she witnessed, do we trust the account, given that we may know little about the source's exposure, bias, and expertise? This is not to assume that people are always intentionally misconstruing the facts. One salient example is police body cameras, which some believe shed light on police encounters but which can be difficult to interpret, and interpretation can be subject to cognitive biases.[16] Even if we extrapolate patterns from the history of a single source's posting, we may not necessarily understand the source's self-censored information. Some people, for example, choose never to mention or show pictures of their children online; others never discuss their work online.

---

[16] Timothy Williams, James Thomas, Samuel Jacoby, and Damien Cave, "Police Body Cameras: What Do You See?" *New York Times*, April 1, 2016.

Contextualizing allows the open source analyst to relay subject-matter expertise to the ultimate consumer. This may involve comments about the source that provide additional information, such as information relevant to credibility. Contextualizing could also involve compiling multiple items of OSIF from any deliverable into a product that provides a more comprehensive picture about an issue.

Production

In the final phase, production, information is provided to a consumer in a usable form. This consumer will most often be an all-source intelligence analyst who is in a position to incorporate it into a multi-intelligence production. However, an open-source product may also be high-priority or complete enough to be provided directly to a policymaker or other intelligence customer. This is akin to other intelligence disciplines, where human, signals, or geospatial intelligence is generally incorporated into an all-source analytic product but at times is provided in its raw form directly to an intelligence customer.[17]

The production phase also includes assigning a classification level to an OSINT product. Although the product may be derived from OSIF, the details of collecting, processing, and exploiting that information may warrant an increased classification level. OSIF may meet a classified intelligence information requirement, particularly when combined with other information.[18] For example, information may be acquired through official or sensitive means, where exposure of the possession of the information would jeopardize its continued accessibility. Open source producers may also use classified processing and exploitation technology that would justify classification of the information.

Dissemination is also a component of the production phase. Open-source analysis is most often disseminated in the form of a written report. However, products may also take the form of verbal briefings or graphic visualizations.

The medium used for dissemination is, unfortunately, often the easiest, rather than the most effective, distribution mechanism. Video, audio, or interactive graphics could often be more effective than written reports for conveying particular information. All-source intelligence analysts generally pull their intelligence reporting from a text-based database, such as Trident, WISE, or Pathfinder. Similarly, intelligence consumers often receive intelligence products in a printed briefing book. However, enhanced capabilities of open-source portals and the transition of the Presidential

---

[17] References to "raw" and "finished" intelligence can sometimes lead to confusion among intelligence professionals. All-source analysts often refer to single-discipline intelligence products as "raw" reporting, even when the product is the result of extensive processing and exploitation. Intelligence collectors often refer to "raw" reporting as the original, unprocessed collected material.

[18] Noah Shachtman, "Open Source Intel Rocks—Sorry, It's Classified," *Wired Magazine*, September 2008.

Daily Brief to an iPad format are paving the way for more creative mechanisms for conveying information, such as data visualizations and dynamic files.

CHAPTER THREE

OSINT Tools and Methods

Challenges of Using Commercial Off-the-Shelf Tools

The IC generally uses commercial off-the-shelf (COTS) tools for OSINT analysis, particularly analysis of social media data. This chapter focuses primarily on existing social media analysis tools. A few important caveats must be kept in mind when considering the utility of these tools for the purposes of intelligence professionals. First and most importantly, most COTS tools are developed for commercial purposes—for advertising, brand management, and consumer analytics. Companies want to understand and predict a customer's buying behavior, to position their product to be available when a customer is most susceptible to influence, and to influence the customer's opinion of the product or the company itself. These tools can often serve the interests of the IC, but they are rarely a perfect match, and many tools have extremely limited utility for the IC because they are not designed for its purposes.

Second, the market developing these tools is so dynamic that it presents problems for the IC. Both COTS tools and the producers developing them are constantly changing. This problem manifests itself in a number of ways.

Data feeds can be limited or eliminated by the company owning the content, for a variety of reasons. Companies may want to protect user data, or conversely, they may start selling user data that were previously available free. Companies may have acquired a capability or developed an indigenous one for social media content analysis, and they may want to undermine competing capabilities by eliminating their data source. For example, Topsy was a social media analytic service that indexed all published Twitter tweets and provided free searching functions. After eight years, the service unexpectedly went offline on December 15, 2015,[1] two years after being acquired by Apple.[2] This case is illustrative for analytics services and IC operations that rely on other services for early phases of the data acquisition and analytic cycle. Apple and

[1] Jordan Valinsky, "Topsy, the Internet's Favorite Social Media Analysis Tool, Has Died at 8," *Digiday*, December 16, 2015.

[2] Daisuke Wakaybayashi and Douglas MacMillan, "Apple Taps Into Twitter, Buying Social Analytics Firm Topsy," *Wall Street Journal*, December 2, 2013.

Topsy provided little information at the time of the acquisition about whether this data feed would remain available, nor did they provide warning before the Topsy platform ultimately went offline.[3] The IC is accustomed to data accesses being unexpectedly unavailable. SIGINT collectors may lose access for a variety of reasons, including system reconfigurations and new encryption. HUMINT collectors grapple with the possibility of a source being compromised or of losing access to subsources or sensitive programs. Satellite malfunctions can leave IMINT collectors in the dark as they arrange repairs. Intelligence consumers may be frustrated by losing a stream of information collected by covert methods, but the loss can be explained as an inevitable consequence of covert methods—the data source is no longer accessible to analyze. One advantage of OSINT is that it is more dependable than covert collection methods. A sudden loss of an open-source data feed—when the raw data are still accessible online—may be unfairly interpreted as reflecting negatively on OSINT by intelligence consumers who may be neither aware of nor interested in the process of transforming raw data into an intelligence deliverable. When Twitter is still online and people are still tweeting, it can be harder to explain to an intelligence consumer why an OSINT product is suddenly no longer available.

The dynamic nature of the social media analytics market is incongruent with the IC's timelines in vetting tools and providers. Figure 3.1 shows possible options available to the IC for using COTS tools. Ideally, the IC would transfer both a data source and an analytic platform to its classified system. The IC, understandably, wants to fully understand an institution and its platform before introducing it to a classified system. By relying on COTS tools, the IC risks being always behind the state of the art in social

Figure 3.1
Possible Options for IC Use of COTS Tools

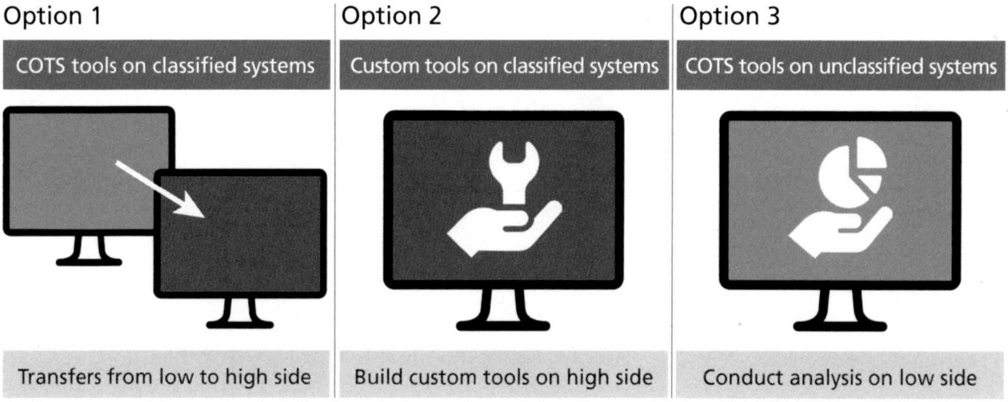

SOURCE: RAND analysis.
RAND *RR1964-3.1*

---

3 Andrew Hutchinson, "Farewell Topsy, You Will Be Missed," *Social Media Today*, December 16, 2015.

media analytics because of the time needed to complete this vetting. The predominance of startup companies in this space complicates the IC's ability to build a trusted relationship with established providers to possibly streamline the vetting process. The IC could, of course, develop indigenous tools, but this is a costly alternative. It could also leverage a tool on an unclassified system and avoid the complication of collocating it with the more-sensitive capabilities and information on classified networks. Social media analytics is also a dynamic market because of rapid improvements in computing power and data-processing capabilities. Tools are becoming more capable of handling large amounts of data, and machine learning is making impressive strides. Instead of humans having to teach computers how to perform complex tasks, systems are being built that enable computers to learn how to conduct these complex tasks themselves.[4]

Methods Used in Social Media Content Analysis

Although the tools for OSINT collection are evolving on a nearly daily basis, the methods used by the tools themselves change less dramatically. Most tools use lexical analysis, network analysis, geospatial analysis, or a combination of these methods to isolate, describe, and analyze data. All three methods existed long before their application to Internet-based content, but the vast proliferation of social media platforms and the ever-increasing ease with which individuals can access the Internet make that environment rich for intelligence collection. Furthermore, just as the transition from Web 1.0 to Web 2.0 has exponentially increased the amount of user-generated data available to parse and analyze for specific characteristics, the transition to Web 3.0—where machine learning and natural language processing will be dominant—is already changing the efficiency of these methods for sorting, translating, and analyzing data for intelligence purposes.

Distinguishing among the proliferating commercially available open-source analytic tools can be difficult, because of their abundance and poor descriptions. Identifying the specific components of the methods they use, however, provides a rubric by which to evaluate and compare capabilities. Tools can be compared in terms of the quantity of analytic methods they can employ and their speed, accuracy, and capacity for performing analyses.

Lexical Analysis

One of the most powerful uses of open source tools in the social media age is the ability to simultaneously aggregate large bodies of text from all over the world at any given time of day from multiple sources across an array of languages, cultures, and nationalities. Lexical analysis can, at its most basic level, show the most searched-for terms

---

4 Alex Hern, "Google Says Machine Learning Is the Future. So I Tried It Myself," *The Guardian*, June 28, 2016.

on Google on any given day or show which keywords appeared most frequently. At a higher level, lexical analysis can parse meaning behind language and infer information about the people engaging in social media, including demographic characteristics such as age, social class, economic background, and education level.[5]

In addition to analytic capabilities, advanced lexical analytic methods are often dependent on having a base corpus for reference. By corpus, in this context, we mean not simply a large collection of text but a comprehensive body of text that provides the basis for the descriptive analysis of a language. While there are well-established corpora available for some languages, including English, Mandarin, and Russian, many languages lack established corpora, and some of the lexical analytic tools cannot be employed until such corpora are created. Machine learning, which is discussed in greater detail later in this chapter, is already helping to overcome some of the language deficits in lexical analysis, and it will continue to improve over time.

Keyness Analysis

Keyness is a measure of how often a word occurs in a given sentence or piece of writing. Keyness analysis can create a vivid picture of a speaker or writer based on the words he or she uses. Certain words appear more often in English-language statements written by native-English speakers than in those written by non-native speakers, for example.[6]

Frequency Profiling

Keyness is also used to determine frequency profiling, i.e., the general ability to either distinguish one corpus from another based on the occurrence of keywords in each body or compare a sample corpus to a large or larger corpus.[7] One application of frequency profiling would be to attribute material to a source, given a sufficient body of confirmed attributed material to reference; it could also be used to differentiate different "phases" in the writing or speech of one person. For example, researchers at Arizona State University used frequency profiling to demonstrate President Ronald Reagan's cognitive decline before he was officially diagnosed with Alzheimer's disease.[8]

---

[5] Luke Sloan, Jeffrey Morgan, Pete Burnap, and Matthew Williams, "Who Tweets? Deriving the Demographic Characteristics of Age, Occupation and Social Class from Twitter User Meta-Data," *PLoS ONE*, Vol. 10, No. 3, 2015.

[6] Sylviane Granger showed a statistically significant underuse of some adverbs ending in *ly* in French non-native English-speaker corpora (Sylviane Granger, "Prefabricated Patterns in Advanced EFL Writing: Collocations and Formulae," *ReseearchGate*, 1998), as described in Justyna Lesniewska and Ewa Witalisz, "Native vs. Non-Native English: Data-Driven Lexical Analysis," *Studia Linguistica Universitatis Lagellonicae Cracoviensis*, Vol. 129, 2012.

[7] Paul Rayson and Roger Garside, "Comparing Corpora Using Frequency Profiling," *Proceedings of the Workshop on Comparing Corpora*, Vol. 9, Association for Computational Linguistics, October 2002.

[8] Visar Berisha, Shuai Wang, Amy LaCross, and Julie M. Liss, "Tracking Discourse Complexity Preceding Alzheimer's Disease Diagnosis: A Case Study Comparing the Press Conferences of Presidents Ronald Reagan and George Herbert Walker Bush," *Journal of Alzheimer's Disease*, Vol. 45, No. 3, 2015, pp. 959–963.

Clusters

A cluster is a sequence of two or more words which may not be a grammatical or meaningful unit in and of itself but which can be included in a keyword analysis.[9]

Collocation

Collocation is the probability that any two of the words identified in a keyness analysis frequently occur together, typically within five words on either side of the word identified for investigation (also referred to as the "node").[10] Collocation can be used not only to enhance search functionality but to help identify key themes in a text. Collocation is important because it can indicate how a person forms connections between concepts. For example, Baker et al., in their study on United Kingdom discourse around refugees, found that four words—immigrant, migrant, refugee, and asylum seeker—shared a consistently high number of collocates, meaning that the United Kingdom press was either intentionally or unintentionally linking those concepts in people's minds.[11]

Sentiment Analysis

Sentiment analysis identifies terms or entities about which a person has "an overall majority opinion which is not shared by a different class," for example, a particular political figure who is seen as divisive.[12] The critical function of sentiment analysis is to take an opinion expressed online and classify it as expressing a positive, negative, or neutral attitude.[13] Sentiment analysis can be employed across a wide range of topics, from the state of American political discourse to the support for ISIS in the Middle East.[14] However, some researchers caution that an overreliance on sentiment analysis risks overstating the role of social media in representing a larger societal voice, rather than representing the percentage of a given population that is online and engaged on a topic.[15]

---

[9] Paul Baker et al., "A Useful Methodological Synergy? Combining Critical Discourse Analysis and Corpus Linguistics to Examine Discourses of Refugees and Asylum Seekers in the UK Press," *Discourse & Society*, Vol. 19, No. 3, 2008, pp. 273–306.

[10] Baker et al., 2008.

[11] Baker et al., 2008, p. 278.

[12] Marco Pennacchiotti and Ana-Maria Popescu, "A Machine Learning Approach to Twitter User Classification," *International AAAI Conference on Weblogs and Social Media*, Sunnyvale, Calif.: Yahoo! Labs, 2011, p. 284.

[13] Katie Cohen, Fredrik Johansson, Lisa Kaati, and Jonas Clausen Mork, "Detecting Linguistic Markers for Radical Violence in Social Media," *Terrorism and Political Violence*, Vol. 26, No. 1, 2014, pp. 245–256.

[14] Cohen et al., 2014.

[15] Mick Endsor and Dr. Bill Peace, "A Call to Arms: Open Source Intelligence and Evidence Based Policymaking," *Bellingcat*, January 20, 2015.

Stance Analysis

While sentiment analysis shows how language can differentiate viewpoints between individuals or groups, stance analysis uses language preferences to indicate an individual's underlying values or an expression of attitude toward a given concept. For example, Marcellino uses stance analysis to show that U.S. Marines speak in a distinct, internally cohesive manner "marked by future-oriented, inclusive, highly certain language."[16]

Natural Language Processing

Previous generations of researchers and intelligence analysts had to rely on human translators and interpreters to process large bodies of text in other languages. Technological advances in text analysis and natural language processing have reduced this burden significantly, and an array of resources is now available for faster translation and processing of foreign-language materials. Some resources, such as Google Translate, are free and open source, and they invite users to offer improved translations for machine-generated text, which in turn improves and fine-tunes the algorithms over time. Cohen et al. note that automatic translation services are "seldom as good as if a human expert had translated the content of a website, but the great advantage with automatic translation is obviously the speed with which large amounts of data can be processed."[17] Speed is an obvious advantage when intelligence analysts are determining how much of a threat an individual posting on an extremist website poses in the immediate future.

Machine Learning

All the lexical-analysis processes and terms described above, from calculating keyness to detecting collocations to translating materials and providing sentiment analysis, are made more efficient through machine learning. Machine learning is the process of teaching a software program to make decisions independent of a human after the desired decisionmaking process has first been modeled extensively for the program. Machine learning requires that experts in both machine learning and computational linguistics initially design the parameters and adequately "teach" the computer how to recognize linguistically relevant patterns in written text.[18]

Applying Lexical Analysis Tools

Using the tools described above, lexical analysis can paint rich pictures of writers, as well as their larger context—the communities they identify with, the individuals or

---

[16] William M. Marcellino, "Talk Like a Marine: USMC Linguistic Acculturation and Civil-Military Argument," *Discourse Studies*, Vol. 16, No. 3, 2014, p. 121.

[17] Cohen et al., 2014, p. 251.

[18] Anna Korhonen, "Automatic Lexical Classification—Balancing Between Machine Learning and Linguistics," in Olivia Kwong, ed., *23rd Pacific Asia Conference on Language, Information, and Computation*, 2009, pp. 19–28.

communities they intend to reach with their words, and possible shifts in ideology or viewpoints over time. Lexical analysis increasingly involves the collection of corpora from the Internet, where people share, post, tweet, and in a myriad of other ways express opinions and share thoughts every day. The use of this method and its application to intelligence collection will almost certainly continue to expand as tools such as natural language processing and machine learning for sentiment and stance analysis continue to improve.

Social Network Analysis

For decades before the advent of the most recent generation of web-based applications, social network analysis attempted to explain the relationships between individuals as a series of exchanges that can be mapped and plotted to explain past and predict future interactions. The underlying principles of social network analysis are the following:[19]

- Actors are viewed as interdependent, not autonomous.
- Relational ties between actors are channels for the transfer or "flow" of resources (either material or nonmaterial).
- Network models view the structural environment as providing opportunities for or constraints on individual action.
- Network models conceptualize structure (social, economic, political, etc.) as lasting patterns of relations among actors.

While social network analysis examines the connections between individuals, the intent is not to explain the individuals but rather to understand the larger network of connected actors. Thus, the unit of examination is larger—dyads (two actors and their relationship), triads (three actors), larger subgroups of individuals, or entire systems.[20] Social network analysis in the Internet age has created an exponential supply of new data points in the study of networked interactions, while new social media tools provide greater visibility into networks.

The foundational elements of social network analysis are presented in Figure 3.2. Each unit in a social network is described as a node. Nodes can be individuals outside of a network or inside, but social network analysis focuses primarily on nodes that are part of larger groups. A dyad is two nodes interacting with each other, as indicated by the line connecting A to B. A triad is similarly an interaction between three nodes—A, B, and C. From these basic building blocks, larger networks form that can describe the ways in which nodes interact with each other, which nodes hold more control or power,

---

[19] Stanley Wasserman and Katherine Faust, *Social Network Analysis: Methods and Applications (Structured Analysis in the Social Sciences)*, Cambridge, UK: Cambridge University Press, 1994.

[20] Robert A. Hanneman and Mark Riddle, *Introduction to Social Network Methods*, Riverside, Calif.: University of California, Riverside, 2005.

and how nodes are linked to each other through shared connections. The star network, line network, and circle network are ways of visualizing different kinds of interactions, which are described with examples below.

Degree

Degree is the number of connections a node has; the larger the degree, the more connections the node has. In Figure 3.2, degree is illustrated by the position of node G in the star network: G has degree six, while all other nodes have degree one, meaning that G will have more opportunities for access to information or greater ability to influence than all the other nodes in the network.

Density

There is a finite number of lines in any graph, and the number of nodes determines the maximum. Density is the ratio of lines that are actually present in the graph to the theoretical possible maximum. In Figure 3.2, the circle network has low density, meaning that there is a low number of lines between the nodes relative to the number that could exist (e.g., A and F could be connected, I and C could be connected). The greater that ratio is, the more interactions occur within a group, which can be mea-

Figure 3.2
Social Network Analysis Diagrams

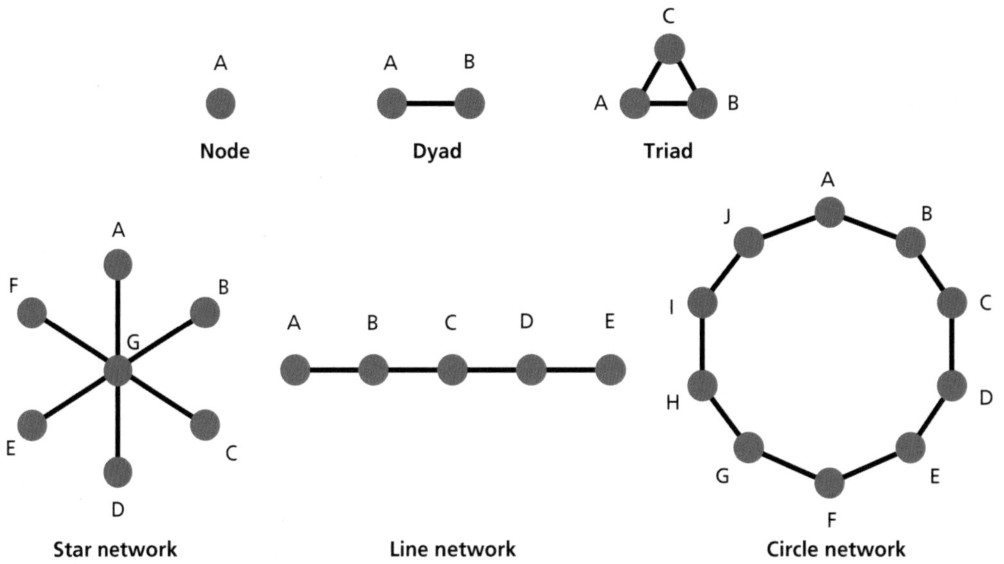

SOURCE: RAND analysis.
RAND *RR1964-3.2*

sured as cohesiveness. Within groups larger than two people, this indicates the "extent to which network members know and interact with each other."[21]

Betweenness

Betweenness is an indication of the degree to which an individual point (or node) controls communication.[22] In the line network in Figure 3.2, B is between A and C; therefore, any information A would like to pass on to C has to travel through B, meaning that B can control the message that C receives, changing that message or preventing it from reaching C entirely. Social network analysis can use measures of betweenness to designate individuals as "influencers" within a given network, seeing how language changes and morphs in the exchange from one actor to the next, as in a giant game of telephone. An important finding for the IC is that betweenness allows researchers to get a vivid idea of what a small number of critical nodes are discussing, even if the users themselves have put up high security protections on their social media presence, if the researchers understand how less-critical actors are connected to that node.[23] In other words, in the giant game of telephone, one can extrapolate what the person in the middle said by determining what the people on either side of him said.

Betweenness Centrality

A corollary to betweenness, betweenness centrality suggests a way to determine how otherwise unassociated networks or individuals share a common link that allows for communication between them. Where two different networks interact—for example, if the star network and the circle network had a shared connection—measures of betweenness centrality indicate how those two groups are linked and provide information on the "heterogeneity or variability of betweenness in the entire set of actors."[24]

Closeness

While betweenness indicates which individuals within a given group might control the message, closeness measures how independent or dependent each individual in a group is from the others and therefore how much any one person depends on another to relay a message.[25] In the line network in Figure 3.2, actor C is closer to all other actors in the network, while actors A and E are farthest away.

---

[21] Catherine A. Heaney and Barbara A. Israel, "Social Networks and Social Support," in Karen Glanz, Barbara K. Rimer, and K. V. Viswanath (eds.), *Health Behavior and Health Education: Theory, Research, and Practice*, Philadelphia: University of Pennsylvania, 2008.

[22] Linton C. Freeman, "Centrality in Social Networks: Conceptual Clarification," *Social Networks*, Vol. 1, 1978/79, pp. 215–239.

[23] Rami Puzis, Dana Yagil, Yuval Elovici,, and Dan Braha, "Collaborative Attack on Internet Users' Anonymity," *Internet Research*, Vol. 19, No. 1, 2009, p. 62.

[24] Puzis et al., 2009, p. 192.

[25] Freeman, 1978/79, p. 225.

Measures of Centrality

Measures of centrality describe an individual node's importance within a larger network. Individuals with high centrality typically have "high involvement in many relations, regardless of send/receive directionality, or volume of activity."[26] In the context of a Twitter interaction, a user with high centrality would frequently get mentioned by other users, regardless of whether the user initiated the conversation or not, and would also frequently initiate interactions with other people in their networks.

Directionality

Measured as "outdegree" (i.e., information going out) or "indegree," (i.e., information coming in), actors with larger indegrees tend to be the most prestigious or important within a network.[27] Directionality, unlike the other measures defined here, looks at where the information originated and in which direction it flows. In the line network, for example, whether a node is important depends on the direction in which information flows; if all information flows to the right, node E would have the largest indegree. In dyads, directionality can indicate whether both members share equal influence/power in the interaction or there is an unequal power dynamic.[28]

Applying Social Network Analysis Tools

Twitter is arguably the most prominent social media tool used by social network analysts to illustrate and investigate classic principles of network analysis. Twitter gives users unique usernames, or "handles," who then use those handles to interact directly with other users by either replying to a publicly available conversation or initiating a conversation with another known user, a process called having "mentions" in a conversation thread. All of these interactions are public. This allows observers to see who interacts with whom, who is connected to whom—and through whom—and the quality and quantity of those interactions.

One example of how social network analysis is currently being employed to understand an issue—and possibly influence its evolution—is the tracking of violent extremist ideology online. Network analysis enables analysts to see how influencers such as ISIS use social media to propagate language and ideology, as well as to identify individuals who may watch an individual YouTube video or read a tweet from a follower and start to engage with the ideas presented. For example, a 2016 RAND study used social media data and lexical analysis to compare ISIS supporters with detractors and determine patterns that provided opportunities for influencing these communities.[29]

---

[26] Chiara Livia Bernardi, *Digital Media and Women's Issues in Egypt and Saudi Arabia*, doctoral thesis, Warwick, UK: University of Warwick, April 2015, p. 139.

[27] Bernardi, 2015, p. 170.

[28] Heaney and Israel, 2008.

[29] Elizabeth Bodine-Baron, Todd Helmus, Madeline Magnuson, and Zev Winkelman, *Examining ISIS Support and Opposition Networks on Twitter*, Santa Monica, Calif.: RAND Corporation, RR-1328-RC, 2016.

By following keywords, or "hashtags," it is possible to track the development of a new keyword and then watch it spread, first between individual users, then into larger networks, and then across networks, possibly taking on a new meaning or definition with each new share. Once a community's patterns of communication and shared language are understood, it may be possible to conduct countermessaging campaigns that use the same keywords that pro-ISIS accounts use to show the negative consequences of becoming involved with the organization. In a recent publication, RAND researchers explored several possibilities for effectively countermessaging ISIS in the Middle East, using a top-down approach on Twitter.[30]

Geospatial Analysis

Like lexical analysis and network analysis, geospatial analysis often works in combination with other methods to produce a richer image of social, military, and political dynamics that are relevant for intelligence collectors. Geospatial analysis has also expanded significantly with the creation of new social media platforms that can automatically link a post or tweet to a specific location through what is known as "geotagging."

Geotagging

Geotags are embedded data that mark the longitude and latitude of a given post or image, with increasingly high levels of accuracy. Most smartphones automatically produce geotags for posts, using their internal Global Positioning System (GPS) location data—for example, on images posted to Instagram—and users of the sites may not realize they have to turn off this default setting in order to not reveal their location.[31] Some users intentionally geotag their posts on Twitter, Facebook, Instagram, Tumblr, and other sites to mark their presence at an event or to help disseminate real-time information on an unfolding event.[32] Goodchild referred to this form of active location collection and dissemination as "volunteered geography," suggesting that the lower cost of GPS-enabled smartphones has lowered the threshold for individual participation.[33]

Volunteered geography is useful for producing information on real-time events and for showing the real-time movement of a group of people into a specific place, for example, the movement of tens of thousands of protesters into Tahrir Square in Cairo, Egypt, during the 2011 protests. Protesters also uploaded videos and images tagged as being in Tahrir Square, which were then picked up by media sources outside of the

---

[30] Todd Helmus and Elizabeth Bodine-Baron, *Empowering ISIS Opponents on Twitter*, Santa Monica, Calif.: RAND Corporation, PE-227-RC, 2017.

[31] Kate Murphy, "Web Photos That Reveal Secrets, Like Where You Live," *New York Times*, August 11, 2010.

[32] "A Twitter Timeline of the Iran Election," *Newsweek*, June 25, 2009.

[33] Michael F. Goodchild, "Citizens as Voluntary Sensors: Spatial Data Infrastructure in the World of Web 2.0," *International Journal of Spatial Data Infrastructure Research*, Vol. 2, No. 1, 2007, pp. 24–32.

country and used to report on ongoing demonstrations and the Egyptian government response. Figure 3.3 is a still-frame map of where geotagged pictures and tweets were posted around Tahrir Square; a series of images would reveal the movement of individuals into the center from surrounding areas, as people posted to social media while in transit to or from the protests. This information can be used to show patterns in movement and trace common paths of entry into protests, events, or gatherings.

The built-in ability in many social media applications to "tag" locations has also revealed a wealth of information. In 2015, a New Zealand man who traveled to Syria to fight with ISIS had his Twitter accounts suspended when he inadvertently sent several geotagged tweets that were specific enough to trace his location to a particular house in al-Taqbah, a Syrian town.[34] Since then, other ISIS fighters in Syria and Iraq have similarly been tracked down through geotagged photos they unintentionally posted on Instagram or Twitter.

Figure 3.3
Map of Tahrir Square with Geotags

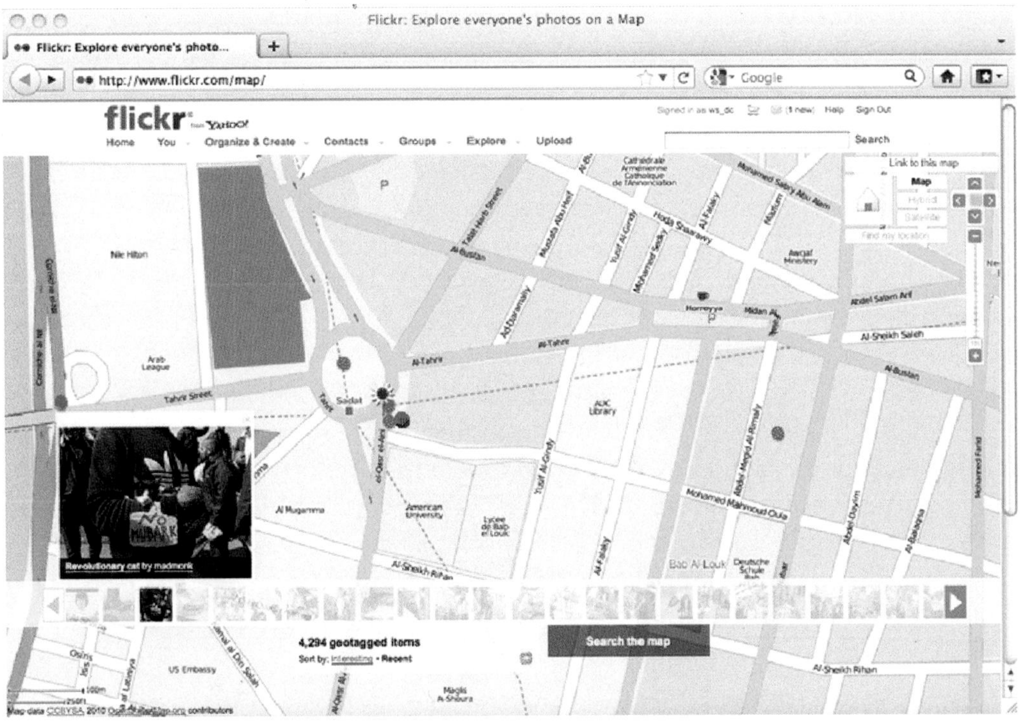

SOURCE: Anthony Stefanidis, Andrew Crooks, and Jacek Radzikowski, "Harvesting Ambient Geospatial Information from Social Media Feeds," *GeoJournal*, Vol. 78, 2013.
RAND *RR1964-3.3*

---

[34] Denver Nicks, "New Zealander ISIS Fighter Accidentally Tweets Secret Location," *Time*, January 1, 2015.

Geolocating

Using open-source programs such as Google Earth and Google Maps, analysts can locate specific landmarks (a church, for example) and then use websites such as Panoramio to combine maps with photographs that have been tagged to a specific location.[35]

Geo-inference

Geo-inference enables the geolocation of a user without explicitly geotagged information. Geo-inference can be done in a variety of ways. Some websites (e.g., Google and Craigslist) record user location in order to customize user experience, which leaves "location-sensitive content" in the cache of the user's browser. Interested parties can access geolocations left in the cache by using "side channels" to determine the user's location, specifically down to the level of neighborhood.[36] On platforms such as Twitter, algorithms are able to take "ambient geospatial information" from the content of the tweets themselves, when the tweets reference location-specific elements such as sports teams or universities.[37] Current versions of these algorithms improve when they have access to more data from any one user, enabling the system to "tweak" its estimation of the user's location based on language use. [38] Cheng, Caverlee, and Lee developed an algorithmic system that examined users with 1,000 or more tweets and located 51 percent of users within 100 miles of their real location, a proportion they state will improve dramatically as they refine the tool with greater data samples.[39]

Georeferencing

Georeferencing associates an object with locations in physical space. It is "commonly used in the geographic information systems field to describe the process of associating a physical map or raster image of a map with spatial locations."[40] When maps have no explicit geographic coordinate system associated with the locations depicted on them, spatial coordinates can be assigned to an image. The image can be overlaid with modern data, which can then be used to create more accurate maps with granular data on infrastructure such as roads and buildings. These maps can later be used for research purposes or, in the intelligence and military communities, for targeting.

---

35 Eliot Higgins, "Geolocation Techniques—Mapping Landmarks," *Bellingcat*, July 15, 2014.

36 Yaoqi Jia, Xinshu Dong, Zhenkai Liang, Prateek Saxena, "I Know Where You've Been: Geo-Inference Attacks via the Browser Cache," National University of Singapore, 2014.

37 Stefanidis, Crooks, and Radzikowski, 2013, pp. 319–338.

38 Zhiyuan Cheng, James Caverlee, and Kyumin Lee, "You Are Where You Tweet: A Content-Based Approach to Geo-locating Twitter Users," *19th ACM International Conference on Information and Knowledge Management*, Toronto, Ontario, Canada, 2010.

39 Cheng, Caverlee, and Lee, 2010.

40 Andreas Hackeloeer, Klaas Klasing, Jukka M. Krisp, and Liqiu Meng, "Georeferencing: A Review of Methods and Applications," *Annals of GIS*, Vol. 20, No. 1, 2014, pp. 61–69.

Applying Geospatial Analysis Tools

One of the powerful uses of geospatial analysis tools is in contextualizing information on a given factor and its effects on infrastructure and population in real time. Software programs such as Geographic Information System allow users to download publicly available maps supported by the Google platform and overlay specific factors of interest—e.g., water resources, population centers over or under a given number, and import data repositories—on factors such as ethnic and religious composition in a region to show interactions between geography and religiosity in an area. Analysts looking at how ongoing military interventions are working in an area can use a combination of Google Maps, Wikimapia, publicly available tweets, Facebook posts, and YouTube videos to pinpoint exact locations of ongoing military actions and their intended and unintended consequences.[41]

This kind of intersectional analysis is illustrated in Figure 3.4, which shows a targeted attack on a convoy of alleged ISIS vehicles near Fallujah, Iraq. The analysis was pulled together by cross-referencing "geolocations of footage released by both the international Coalition and the Iraqi Ministry of Defence, official statements, and media reports."[42] By placing all the available information on a map that can be updated and edited as new information comes in, geospatial analytics becomes a powerful tool for visualizing and analyzing intelligence reports.

Geospatial, social network, and lexical analysis, when paired with an ever-expanding list of private and public software platforms, are increasingly helping to make sense of big data problems and to separate signal from noise. The possibilities offered by machine learning and natural language processing are enormous for OSINT collection. At the same time, it will remain critical for intelligence analysts to play a role in determining how to connect the information offered by these methods in a way that is compelling and reliable. Making sense of the kind of data collected by each method will also require intelligence analysts to form connections with scholars and scientists outside of their fields, particularly in the areas of computer science, including experts at technology companies and specialists in linguistics, sociology, and other relevant areas. While machine learning will increasingly replace some time-consuming collection and processing tasks, skilled analysts will still be needed to create compelling narratives from their data.

---

[41] Christiaan Triebert, "An Open Source Analysis of the Fallujah 'Convoy Massacre'(s)," *Bellingcat*, July 6, 2016.

[42] Triebert, 2016.

Figure 3.4
A Targeted Attack on a Convoy of Alleged ISIS Vehicles Near Fallujah, Iraq

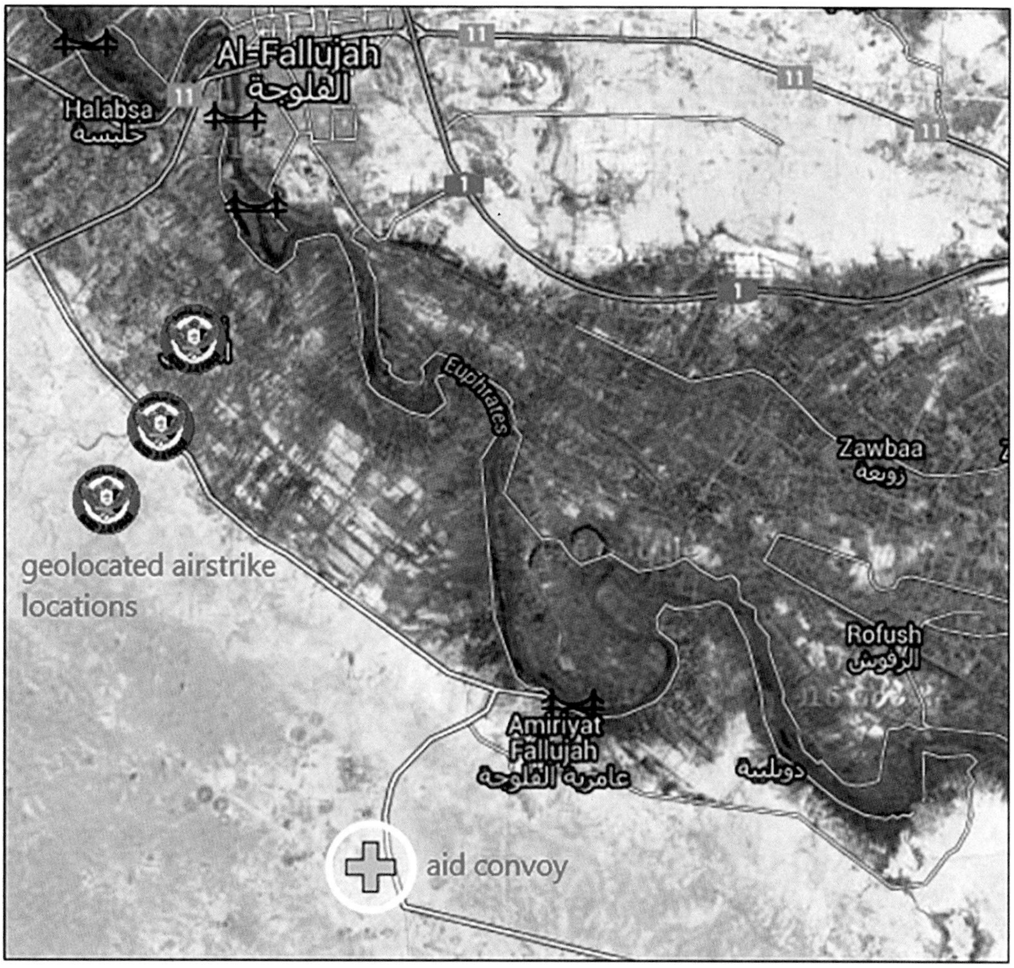

SOURCE: Triebert, 2016.
RAND *RR1964-3.4*

for the first time every second. Seven people use a mobile phone for the first time every second. One million people will use the Internet for the first time today." He went on to challenge the conference attendees: "I challenge you to reject complacency, nurture innovation, and create an environment for the technology that will allow the IC to collect analyze and deliver intelligence to the customer needed to cope with the changes of the 21st century."[5] DIA has been looking at how to better identify, hire, and organize data scientists, a de facto recognition this cadre does not currently exist among its workforce.[6] DoD Instruction 3115.12 established the Defense Open Source Council and designated DIA as "the primary governance mechanism for DoD OSINT."[7] The chair of the Defense Open Source Council is a DIA official who guides the council's work support DoD OSINT activities.

Organizations are attempting to figure out how to incorporate and integrate OSIF. However, these are tweaks more than transformations. Rethinking how the IC would ideally be organized into disciplines today regardless of the current organizational framework—even if reshaping the community entirely would be too prohibitive, given institutional cultures, legacies, workforce tolerance for change, and practical necessities—could still provide insightful and novel recommendations for the IC.

Third-Generation OSINT?

As the IC continues to grapple with how to manage and fully exploit second-generation OSINT, it is useful to think about where the web is going next and the trends that could define a third generation of OSINT. Second-generation OSINT evolved largely because of Web 2.0—a shift in Internet context to dynamic web pages and user-generated content. For more than a decade, however, technology experts have talked about the evolution to Web 3.0—the "Semantic Web"—which would include direct and indirect machine processing of data, machine learning, and automated reasoning.[8] Figure 4.1 presents some of the characteristics of OSINT generations and possibilities for the next wave of challenges and focus.

The volume of available data could potentially be offset by new data storage and processing capabilities if the IC is effectively positioned for such an evolution. For example, live video and broadcasting is becoming increasingly common. In 2011, You-

---

[5] Jim Hodges, "DIA Seeks Culture Sift," *Trajectory Magazine*, June 7, 2017.

[6] Bradley Knopp, Sina Beaghley, Aaron Frank, Rebeca Orrie, and Michael Watson, "Defining the Roles, Responsibilities, and Functions for Data Science Within the Defense Intelligence Agency," Santa Monica, Calif.: RAND Corporation, RR-1582-DIA, 2016.

[7] Department of Defense Instruction 3115.12, "Open Source Intelligence (OSINT)," Washington, D.C., August 24, 2010.

[8] John Markoff, "Entrepreneurs See a Web Guided by Common Sense," *New York Times*, November 12, 2006.

Figure 4.1
Characteristics of OSINT Generations

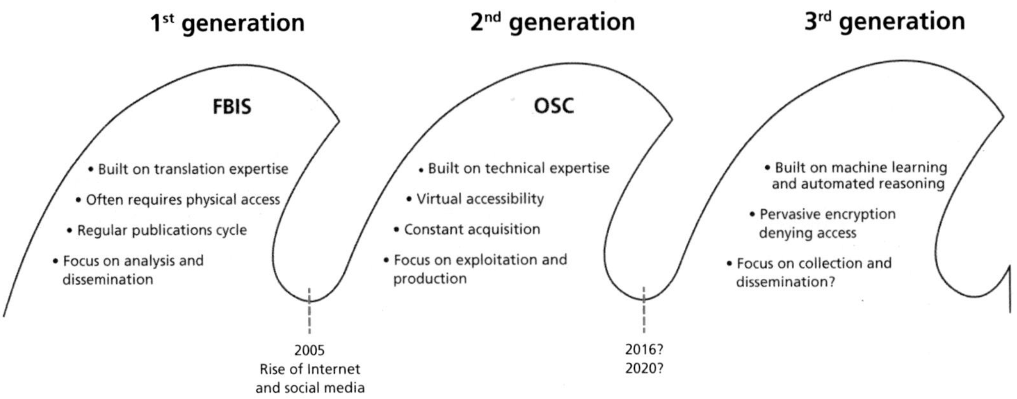

SOURCE: RAND analysis.
RAND *RR1964-4.1*

Tube was already uploading more video content in a 60-day period than was ever created by the three major U.S. television networks.[9] By 2015, 300 hours of video were being uploaded to YouTube every minute.[10] Multiple new platforms provide users with the opportunity to broadcast live video.[11] Live video could give the IC real-time awareness of ongoing events; however, without the use of computer analysis, it would not be possible to process this large volume of information in real time.

The conversation on OSINT often focuses on intelligence analysis; however, there is a potentially equal or greater opportunity for intelligence operations. One example is augmented reality—where a digital layer "augments" reality—and wearable technology.[12] Well-known examples of automated reality are Google Glass, an optical display in the shape of eyeglasses that displays digital information, and Pokemon Go, a game that overlays digital images on the real world, using GPS-enabled smartphones. Augmented reality technology could have potential for targeting and recruitment of human assets for HUMINT operations.

Psychometrics—a "data-driven sub-branch of psychology"[13]—also holds potential to further blur the line between OSINT and psychological and information operations. For example, technology firm Cambridge Analytica claims to be able to pre-

---

9 Amy-Mae Turner, "10 Fascinating YouTube Facts That May Surprise You," *Mashable*, February 19, 2011.

10 "YouTube Statistics," March 17, 2015.

11 Elise Moreau, "10 Popular Tools for Broadcasting Live Video Online," *Lifewire*, October 2, 2016.

12 Dan Farber, "The Next Big Thing in Tech: Augmented Reality," *CNET*, June 7, 2013.

13 Hannes Grassegger and Mikael Krogerus, "The Data That Turned the World Upside Down," *Motherboard*, January 28, 2017.

dict individual behavior based on publicly available data points and data modeling.[14] According to the *National Review*, the firm was employed by 2016 U.S. presidential campaigns to create political advertisements with messages crafted to target unconscious biases.[15] This technology not only holds potential for intelligence operations, it raises new questions about ethics and legal authorities for the IC.

Encryption is also likely to become a more prevalent characteristic of third-generation OSINT, as encryption software becomes increasingly pervasive, accessible, and robust. The online magazine *Wired* has described 2016 as "the year encryption won," evidenced by the increasing use of end-to-end encryption by ordinary users and a legal challenge over encryption between Apple and the Federal Bureau of Investigation.[16] As encryption becomes mainstream, it raises new definitional and division-of-labor issues for the IC. Decryption of information for potential intelligence value has generally fallen under the purview of NSA and its SIGINT mandate; however, traditionally, government agencies were the users of encryption technologies. If users who produce information that is currently considered OSINT begin using encryption, will the IC now consider that information SIGINT and transfer responsibility for its exploitation to NSA?

Conclusion

There are many opportunities for further research into OSINT methodology, COTS tools for open-source analysis, and open-source analytic methods to bring greater intelligence value to the IC and to enable more-efficient operations. For example, as mentioned in Chapter Two, a rigorous evaluation of the difficulty of the OSINT methodological cycle for different OSINT subtypes could provide for a better division of resources and effort among various OSINT sources. This could be gauged by interviewing open source professionals and measuring the time and effort expended in producing a broad sample of OSINT projects. The IC could also benefit greatly from additional work on analytic methods and existing analytic tools, as discussed in Chapter Three. For instance, existing COTS tools could be evaluated against the methods identified in Chapter Three. These tools could also be evaluated on practical measures such as cost, ease of use, transparency of methods, and understandability of outputs for IC consumers. A living database of the various platforms could assist the IC offices that have an OSINT function, enabling them to spend resources wisely and avoid redundancies. Further, the fixation of COTS tools on short-form social media content

---

14 Cambridge Analytica, "Data Drives All We Do," undated.

15 Eliana Johnson, "Trump Campaign Turns to 'Psychographic' Data Firm Used by Cruz," *National Review*, August 5, 2016.

16 Brian Barrett, "The Year Encryption Won," *Wired*, December 23, 2016.

analysis distracts from the opportunities provided by expanded IC exploitation of gray literature and long-form social media content. It would be productive to evaluate the allocation of IC resources between the four types of OSIF defined in this report and to explore areas where data science and analytic tools could enhance the IC's use of all types of OSIF.

Finally, the IC could expand its partnership with private industry and academia, both of which have always operated in the open-source domain and mature their capabilities as the digital revolution continues to evolve and expand. Outreach to nongovernmental entities poses some challenges for IC organizations, but these challenges are manageable. Existing impediments to collaboration with nongovernmental innovators on data collection and big data analytics need to be overcome. Making this outreach a priority through policy changes and funding allocations is an important first step to furthering existing partnerships, creating new ones, and ensuring the IC stays current in a rapidly changing domain.

References

Ackerman, Robert K., "The CIA Accelerates Innovation," *Signal*, June 1, 2016. As of June 22, 2017: http://www.afcea.org/content/?q=Article-cia-accelerates-innovation

Allen, Deane J., and Brian G. Shellum (eds.), *Defense Intelligence Agency: At the Creation, 1961–1965*, Washington, D.C.: Defense Intelligence Agency, January 2002.

Baker, Paul, et al., "A Useful Methodological Synergy? Combining Critical Discourse Analysis and Corpus Linguistics to Examine Discourses of Refugees and Asylum Seekers in the UK Press," *Discourse & Society*, Vol. 19, No. 3, 2008, pp. 273–306. As of June 22, 2017: http://www.research.lancs.ac.uk/portal/en/publications/a-useful-methodological-synergy-combining-critical-discourse-analysis-and-corpus-linguistics-to-examine-discourses-of-refugees-and-asylum-seekers-in-the-uk-press(97de51f8-d9e4-470e-bd3f-742db873e592)/export.html

Barber, Ben, "CIA Media Translations May Be Cut: Users Rush to Save Valuable Resource," *Washington Times*, December 30, 1996. As of June 22, 2017: https://fas.org/irp/fbis/washtime.html

Barrett, Brian, "The Year Encryption Won," *Wired*, December 23, 2016.

Benes, Libor, "OSINT, New Technologies, Education: Expanding Opportunities and Threats. A New Paradigm," *Journal of Strategic Security*, Vol. 6, No. 5, Fall 2013, p. 25.

Berisha, Visar, Shuai Wang, Amy LaCross, and Julie M. Liss, "Tracking Discourse Complexity Preceding Alzheimer's Disease Diagnosis: A Case Study Comparing the Press Conferences of Presidents Ronald Reagan and George Herbert Walker Bush," *Journal of Alzheimer's Disease*, Vol. 45, No. 3, 2015, pp. 959–963.

Bernardi, Chiara Livia, *Digital Media and Women's Issues in Egypt and Saudi Arabia*, doctoral thesis, Warwick, UK: University of Warwick, April 2015, p. 139.

Best, Richard A., Jr., and Alfred Cumming, *Open Source Intelligence (OSINT): Issues for Congress*, Washington, D.C.: Congressional Research Service, December 2007. As of June 22, 2017: https://www.fas.org/sgp/crs/intel/RL34270.pdf

Cambridge Analytica, "Data Drives All We Do," undated. As of June 22, 2017: https://cambridgeanalytica.org

Cameron, Darla, and Nancy Scola, "Mapping the World's 4.3 Billion Internet Addresses," *The Washington Post*, January 7, 2015. As of June 22, 2017: https://www.washingtonpost.com/graphics/business/world-ip-addresses/

Central Intelligence Agency, "Establishment of the DNI Open Source Center," *News and Information*, November 8, 2005. As of June 22, 2017: https://www.cia.gov/news-information/press-releases-statements/press-release-archive-2005/pr11082005.html

Cheng, Zhiyuan, James Caverlee, and Kyumin Lee, "You Are Where You Tweet: A Content-Based Approach to Geo-locating Twitter Users," *19th ACM International Conference on Information and Knowledge Management*, Toronto, Ontario, Canada, 2010.

Cohen, Katie, Fredrik Johansson, Lisa Kaati, and Jonas Clausen Mork, "Detecting Linguistic Markers for Radical Violence in Social Media," *Terrorism and Political Violence*, Vol. 26, No. 1, pp. 245–256. As of June 22, 2017:
http://www.tandfonline.com/doi/abs/10.1080/09546553.2014.849948

Colquhoun, Cameron, "A Brief History of Open Source Intelligence," *Bellingcat*, July 14, 2016. As of June 22, 2017:
https://www.bellingcat.com/resources/articles/2016/07/14/a-brief-history-of-open-source-intelligence/

Department of Defense Instruction 3115.12, "Open Source Intelligence (OSINT)," Washington, D.C., August 24, 2010. As of April 10, 2018:
https://fas.org/irp/doddir/dod/i3115_12.pdf

"Deputy Director Cohen Delivers Remarks on CIA of the Future at Cornell University," *News and Information*, Washington, D.C.: Central Intelligence Agency, September 17, 2015. As of June 22, 2017:
https://www.cia.gov/news-information/speeches-testimony/2015-speeches-testimony/deputy-director-cohen-delivers-remarks-on-cia-of-the-future-at-cornell-university.html

Director of National Intelligence Open Source Center Implementation Plan, November 1, 2005. As of June 22, 2017:
http://www.osif.us/images/DNI_Open_Source_Center_Implementation_Plan-2005-11-031.doc

Director of National Intelligence, "National Open Source Enterprise," Intelligence Community Directive Number 301, effective July 11, 2006. As of November 10, 2017:
https://www.hsdl.org/?view&did=469452

Endsor, Mick, and Dr. Bill Peace, "A Call to Arms: Open Source Intelligence and Evidence Based Policymaking," *Bellingcat*, January 20, 2015. As of June 22, 2017:
https://www.bellingcat.com/resources/articles/2015/01/20/a-call-to-arms-open-source-intelligence-and-evidence-based-policymaking/

"Establishment of the DNI Open Source Center," *News and Information*, Washington, D.C.: Central Intelligence Agency, November 8, 2005. As of June 22, 2017:
https://www.cia.gov/news-information/press-releases-statements/press-release-archive-2005/pr11082005.html

Farber, Dan, "The Next Big Thing in Tech: Augmented Reality," *CNET*, June 7, 2013. As of June 22, 2017:
https://www.cnet.com/news/the-next-big-thing-in-tech-augmented-reality/

Freeman, Linton C., "Centrality in Social Networks: Conceptual Clarification," *Social Networks*, Vol. 1, 1978/79, pp. 215–239.

Goodchild, Michael F., "Citizens as Voluntary Sensors: Spatial Data Infrastructure in the World of Web 2.0," *International Journal of Spatial Data Infrastructure Research*, Vol. 2, No. 1, pp. 24–32. As of June 22, 2017:
http://ijsdir.jrc.ec.europa.eu/index.php/ijsdir/article/view/28

Granger, S., "Prefabricated Patterns in Advanced EFL Writing: Collocations and Formulae," in A. P. Cowie (ed.), *Phraseology: Theory, Analysis, and Applications*, Oxford, UK: Oxford University Press, 1998, pp. 145–160.

Grassegger, Hannes, and Mikael Krogerus, "The Data That Turned the World Upside Down," *Motherboard*, January 28, 2017. As of June 22, 2017:
https://motherboard.vice.com/en_us/article/how-our-likes-helped-trump-win

Hanneman, Robert A., and Mark Riddle, *Introduction to Social Network Methods,* Riverside, Calif.: University of California, Riverside, 2005. As of June 22, 2017:
http://www.faculty.ucr.edu/~hanneman/nettext/

Heaney, Catherine A., and Barbara A. Israel, "Social Networks and Social Support," in Karen Glanz, Barbara K. Rimer, and K. V. Viswanath (eds.), *Health Behavior and Health Education: Theory, Research, and Practice*, Philadelphia: University of Pennsylvania, 2008. As of June 22, 2017:
http://www.med.upenn.edu/hbhe4/part3-ch9-key-constructs-social-networks.shtml

Helmus, Todd, and Elizabeth Bodine-Baron, *Empowering ISIS Opponents on Twitter*, Santa Monica, Calif.: RAND Corporation, PE-227-RC, 2017. As of July 31, 2017:
https://www.rand.org/pubs/perspectives/PE227.html

Hern, Alex, "Google Says Machine Learning Is the Future. So I Tried It Myself," *The Guardian*, June 28, 2016. As of June 22, 2017:
https://www.theguardian.com/technology/2016/jun/28/
google-says-machine-learning-is-the-future-so-i-tried-it-myself

Higgins, Eliot, "Geolocation Techniques—Mapping Landmarks," *Bellingcat*, July 15, 2014. As of June 22, 2017:
https://www.bellingcat.com/resources/how-tos/2014/07/15/
geolocation-techniques-mapping-landmarks/

Hoffman, Mary-Louise, "Robert Cardillo: NGA Forms New Strategy to Accelerate Interoperability in GEOINT Enterprise System," *ExecutiveGov*, May 17, 2016. As of June 22, 2017:
http://www.executivegov.com/2016/05/robert-cardillo-nga-forms-new-strategy-to-accelerate-interoperability-in-geoint-enterprise-system/

Hodges, Jim, "DIA Seeks Culture Sift," Trajectory Magazine, June 7, 2017. As of April 10, 2018:
http://trajectorymagazine.com/dia-seeks-culture-shift/

Hulnick, Arthur S., "The Dilemma of Open Source Intelligence: Is OSINT Really Intelligence?" in Loch K. Johnson (ed.), *The Oxford Handbook of National Security Intelligence*, New York: Oxford University Press, 2010.

Hutchinson, Andrew, "Farewell Topsy, You Will Be Missed," *Social Media Today*, December 16, 2015. As of June 22, 2017:
http://www.socialmediatoday.com/technology-data/farewell-topsy-you-will-be-missed

Intelligence Reform and Terrorism Prevention Act of 2004, Sec. 1052, pp. 166–167. As of June 22, 2017:
https://www.ise.gov/sites/default/files/IRTPA_amended.pdf

Jia, Yaoqi, Xinshu Dong, Zhenkai Liang, and Prateek Saxena, "I Know Where You've Been: Geo-Inference Attacks via the Browser Cache," National University of Singapore. As of June 22, 2017:
https://www.comp.nus.edu.sg/~jiayaoqi/publications/geo_inference.pdf

Johnson, Eliana, "Trump Campaign Turns to 'Psychographic' Data Firm Used by Cruz," *National Review,* August 5, 2016. As of June 22, 2017:
http://www.nationalreview.com/article/438739/
trump-campaigns-data-firm-partner-cambridge-analytica-worked-cruz

Johnson, Loch K. (ed.), *Handbook of Intelligence Studies*, New York: Routledge, 2007, p. 132.

Joint Chiefs of Staff, *Intelligence Community Directive Number 301: National Open Source Enterprise*, July 11, 2006. As of June 22, 2017:
https://fas.org/irp/dni/icd/icd-301.pdf

———, *JCAT: Intelligence Guide for First Responders*, McLean, Va.: National Counterterrorism Center, 2013.

———, *Joint Publication 2-0: Joint Intelligence*, October 22, 2013, p. B-7. As of June 22, 2017:
http://www.dtic.mil/doctrine/new_pubs/jp2_0.pdf

Kempster, Norman, "Academia Mounts Fight to Save a CIA Program," *Los Angeles Times*, January 14, 1997. As of June 22, 2017:
http://articles.latimes.com/1997-01-14/news/mn-18544_1_foreign-broadcasts

Knopp, Bradley, Sina Beaghley, Aaron Frank, Rebeca Orrie, and Michael Watson, "Defining the Roles, Responsibilities, and Functions for Data Science Within the Defense Intelligence Agency," Santa Monica, Calif.: RAND Corporation, RR-1582-DIA, 2016. As of June 22, 2017:
http://www.rand.org/pubs/research_reports/RR1582.html

Korhonen, Anna, "Automatic Lexical Classification—Balancing Between Machine Learning and Linguistics," in Olivia Kwong (ed.), *23rd Pacific Asia Conference on Language, Information, and Computation*, Hong Kong: City University of Hong Kong, 2009, pp. 19–28.

Lesniewska, Justyna, and Ewa Witalisz, "Native vs. Non-Native English: Data-Driven Lexical Analysis," *Studia Linguistica Universitatis Lagellonicae Cracoviensis,* Vol. 129, 2012.

Lowenthal, Mark M., "OSINT: The State of the Art, The Artless State," *Studies in Intelligence*, Vol. 45, No. 3, 2001, released September 5, 2014, p. 63. As of June 22, 2017:
https://www.cia.gov/library/readingroom/document/0006122548

Manley, Craig, "Managing Army Open Source Activities," *Military Intelligence,* Vol. 31, No. 4, October–December 2005, p. 10. As of June 22, 2017:
https://fas.org/irp/agency/army/mipb/2005_04.pdf

Marcellino, William M., "Talk Like a Marine: USMC Linguistic Acculturation and Civil-Military Argument," *Discourse Studies*, Vol. 16, No. 3, 2014. As of June 22, 2017:
http://www.academia.edu/3831158/Talk_Like_a_Marine_USMC_Linguistic_Acculturation_and_Civil_Military_Argument

Markoff, John, "Entrepreneurs See a Web Guided by Common Sense," *New York Times,* November 12, 2006. As of June 22, 2017:
http://www.nytimes.com/2006/11/12/business/12web.html

Mercado, Stephen C., "Sailing the Sea of OSINT in the Information Age: A Vulnerable Source in a New Era," *Studies in Intelligence*, Vol. 48, No. 3, 2004. As of June 22, 2017:
https://www.cia.gov/library/center-for-the-study-of-intelligence/csi-publications/csi-studies/studies/vol48no3/article05.html

Moreau, Elise, "10 Popular Tools for Broadcasting Live Video Online," *Lifewire,* October 2, 2016. As of June 22, 2017:
https://www.lifewire.com/tools-for-broadcasting-live-video-3486110

Murphy, Kate, "Web Photos That Reveal Secrets, Like Where You Live," *New York Times*, August 11, 2010. As of June 22, 2017:
http://www.nytimes.com/2010/08/12/technology/personaltech/12basics.html

National Counterterrorism Center, *JCAT: Intelligence Guide for First Responders*, p. 20. As of June 22, 2017:
https://www.nctc.gov/jcat/docs/Intelligence_Guide_for_First_Responders.pdf

Nicks, Denver, "New Zealander ISIS Fighter Accidentally Tweets Secret Location," *Time*, January 1, 2015. As of June 22, 2017:
http://time.com/3651559/new-zealand-isis-twitter/

Office of the Director of National Intelligence, "What Is Intelligence?" undated. As of June 22, 2017:
https://www.dni.gov/index.php/what-we-do/what-is-intelligence

Office of the Director of National Intelligence, *U.S. National Intelligence: An Overview 2011*, Washington, D.C., 2011. As of November 10, 2017:
https://www.dni.gov/files/documents/IC_Consumers_Guide_2011.pdf

O'Reilly, Tim, "What Is Web 2.0: Design Patterns and Business Models for the Next Generation of Software," *O'Reilly*, September 30, 2005. As of June 22, 2017:
http://www.oreilly.com/pub/a/web2/archive/what-is-web-20.html

Pennacchiotti, Marco, and Ana-Maria Popescu, "A Machine Learning Approach to Twitter User Classification," *International AAAI Conference on Weblogs and Social Media*, Sunnyvale, Calif.: Yahoo Labs, 2011, p. 284.

Public Law 109-163, National Defense Authorization Act for Fiscal Year 2006, Sec. 931, Department of Defense Strategy for Open-Source Intelligence, January 6, 2006.

Puzis, Rami, Dana Yagil, Yuval Elovici, and Dan Braha, "Collaborative Attack on Internet Users' Anonymity," *Internet Research*, Vol. 19, No. 1, 2009, p. 62. As of June 22, 2017:
http://necsi.edu/affiliates/braha/Internet_Research_Anonimity.pdf

Quinn, Kristin, "Interview with NGA Director Robert Cardillo: NGA Director Robret Cardillo Shares His Vision for the Future," *TrajectoryMagazine.com*, No. 4, 2014. As of June 22, 2017:
http://trajectorymagazine.com/trajectory-mag/item/1858-interview-with-nga-director-robert-cardillo.html

Rayson, Paul, and Roger Garside, "Comparing Corpora Using Frequency Profiling," *Proceedings of the Workshop on Comparing Corpora*, Vol. 9, Association for Computational Linguistics, October 2002.

Riddel, J. Niles, *Remarks at the First International Symposium 'National Security and National Competitiveness: Open Source Solutions*,'" December 2, 1992. As of June 22, 2017:
https://fas.org/irp/fbis/riddel.html

Roop, Joseph E., *Foreign Broadcast Information Service. History.* Part I: *1941–1947*, Washington, D.C.: Central Intelligence Agency, April 1969, p. 7. As of June 22, 2017:
http://www.dtic.mil/dtic/tr/fulltext/u2/a510770.pdf

Shachtman, Noah, "Open Source Intel Rocks—Sorry, It's Classified," *Wired*, September 2008. As of June 22, 2017:
https://www.wired.com/2008/09/download-hayden/

Slick, Stephen, "Measuring Change at the CIA," *Foreign Policy*, May 4, 2016. As of June 22, 2017:
http://foreignpolicy.com/2016/05/04/measuring-change-at-the-cia/

Sloan, Luke, Jeffrey Morgan, Pete Burnap, and Matthew Williams, "Who Tweets? Deriving the Demographic Characteristics of Age, Occupation and Social Class from Twitter User Meta-Data," *PLoS ONE*, Vol. 10, No. 3, 2015. As of June 22, 2017:
http://journals.plos.org/plosone/article?id=10.1371/journal.pone.0115545

Soule, Mason H., and R. Paul Ryan, *Gray Literature*, Fort Belvoir, Va.: Defense Technical Information Center, August 10, 1995. As of June 22, 2017:
http://www.dtic.mil/dtic/tr/fulltext/u2/b300928.pdf

Stefanidis, Anthony, Andrew Crooks, and Jacek Radzikowski, "Harvesting Ambient Geospatial Information from Social Media Feeds," *GeoJournal*, Vol. 78, 2013, pp. 319–338.

Studeman, Admiral William, *Teaching the Giant to Dance: Contradictions and Opportunities in Open Source Within the Intelligence Community*, Open Source Solutions, Inc., December 1992. As of June 22, 2017:
https://fas.org/irp/fbis/studem.html

Swarts, Phillip, "How the NGA Is Learning to Stop Worrying and Love Open-Source Data," *SpaceNews Magazine*, December 19, 2016. As of June 22, 2017:
http://www.spacenewsmag.com/feature/how-the-nga-is-learning-to-stop-worrying-and-love-open-source-data/

Triebert, Christiaan, "An Open Source Analysis of the Fallujah 'Convoy Massacre'(s)," *Bellingcat*, July 6, 2016. As of June 22, 2017:
https://www.bellingcat.com/news/mena/2016/07/06/an-open-source-analysis-of-the-fallujah-convoy-massacres/

Turner, Amy-Mae, "10 Fascinating YouTube Facts That May Surprise You," *Mashable,* February 19, 2011. As of June 22, 2017:
http://mashable.com/2011/02/19/youtube-facts/#xf8QQbKRbGqY

"A Twitter Timeline of the Iran Election," *Newsweek*, 2009. As of June 22, 2017:
http://www.newsweek.com/2009/06/25/a-twitter-timeline-of-the-iran-election.html

U.S. Department of Defense, Department of Defense Instruction 3115.12, Washington, D.C., August 24, 2010. As of June 22, 2017:
http://www.dtic.mil/whs/directives/corres/pdf/311512p.pdf

Valinsky, Jordan, "Topsy, the Internet's Favorite Social Media Analysis Tool, Has Died at 8," *Digiday*, December 16, 2015. As of June 22, 2017:
http://digiday.com/brands/topsy-the-internets-favorite-social-media-analysis-tool-has-died-at-8/

Wakaybayashi, Daisuke, and Douglas MacMillan, "Apple Taps Into Twitter, Buying Social Analytics Firm Topsy," *The Wall Street Journal*, December 2, 2013. As of June 22, 2017:
http://www.wsj.com/articles/SB10001424052702304854804579234450633315742

Wasserman, Stanley, and Katherine Faust, *Social Network Analysis: Methods and Applications*, Cambridge, UK: Cambridge University Press, 1994.

Williams, Timothy, James Thomas, Samuel Jacoby, and Damien Cave, "Police Body Cameras: What Do You See?" *New York Times*, April 1, 2016. As of June 22, 2017:
https://www.nytimes.com/interactive/2016/04/01/us/police-bodycam-video.html

YouTube Statistics, March 17, 2015. As of June 22, 2017:
https://web.archive.org/web/20150317201335/https://www.youtube.com/yt/press/statistics.html